NEIGHBOURS
and other plays
by James Saunders

ANDRE DEUTSCH

FIRST PUBLISHED 1968 BY
ANDRE DEUTSCH LIMITED
105 GREAT RUSSELL STREET
LONDON WCI
COPYRIGHT © 1968 BY JAMES SAUNDERS
ALL RIGHTS RESERVED
PRINTED IN GREAT BRITAIN BY
THE GARDEN CITY PRESS LIMITED
LETCHWORTH, HERTFORDSHIRE
SBN 233 96030 9

H 2 4 NOV 1969

CONTENTS

To Laurence

NEIGHBOURS

First performance at the Questors Theatre, Ealing, October 1964

WOMAN	Ffrangcon Whelan
MAN	Wyllie Longmore

Directed by ALAN CLARKE

First professional performance in Great Britain at the Hampstead Theatre Club on May 8, 1967, in a double bill with LeRoi Jones' *Dutchman*. Subsequently it transferred to the Mayfair Theatre. It had the following cast:

WOMAN	Toby Robins
MAN	Calvin Lockhart

Directed by CHARLES JARROTT

Designed by PATRICK DOWNING

NEIGHBOURS

[*A room. A young* WOMAN *sits reading a book.*
After a while there is a knock at the door. The WOMAN *looks up.*
There is a slight pause before she says:]

WOMAN: Come in.

[*The door opens and a young* MAN *enters. He is a negro. He stops*
just inside the room, his hand on the door handle.]

MAN: Hallo.
WOMAN: Hallo. [*She has stood up on seeing him.*]
MAN: Don't get up.
WOMAN: I'm up.
MAN: Yeah. Well in that case sit down.

[*He laughs, partly to cover the fact that in his nervousness it sounded*
too much like an order. But she remains standing as he quickly
follows the laugh.]

Am I disturbing you? I mean interrupting anything?
WOMAN: No, I was just having some coffee—
MAN: No, I mean you were reading—
WOMAN: It's quite all right, really. . . .

[*He seems to ponder this for a moment.*]

MAN: Hm. . . . [*He backs up against the door, without looking at it, his*
hand still on the handle, until it closes.] In that case I'll come in.
[*Slight pause.*] Sit down, please, please sit down.

[*She does so, not yet feeling it necessary to ask him to. He remains*
for the moment by the door.]

Sorry, you *do* want the door closed? Sure, it was closed when
I came in, wasn't it?
WOMAN: Yes.

MAN: That is, *before* I came in. Hm?

[*She smiles, faintly.*]

Only some people like to leave their doors open—say, you do know me, don't you?

WOMAN [*smiling*]: Yes, of course I do—

MAN: Fourth floor; I just wondered—

WOMAN: We've been nodding to one another long enough.

MAN: Yeah, sure, that's a fact. It just occurred to me, only you know people can look different close up—you know?

WOMAN: We've passed on the stairs; that's close enough.

MAN: How d'you mean? Oh, sure, that's close enough.

WOMAN: I know what you mean though.

MAN: You do. [*A pause.*] You want to know what I'm doing here; the way it is, I want to consult you about something.

WOMAN: Consult me?

MAN: Sure. I want your advice, you see, on a matter.

WOMAN: Oh, I see; I'll be glad to help you if I can.

MAN: Mhm.

WOMAN: Though I'm afraid I don't know much about anything; I mean I'm not very knowledgeable. [*Slight pause.*] Would you like to sit down?

MAN [*immediately*]: Thanks, I'm sure; it's very kind of you; I was wondering when you were going to ask me. [*He is by now sitting. He laughs.*] I see that's a rocking chair you've got there.

WOMAN: Yes, it is.

MAN: I thought rocking chairs were old-fashioned; but that's a new chair, isn't it?

WOMAN: I've had it a little while. They make them nowadays. I mean contemporary ones.

MAN: They do? That's great. I must go out and get myself a contemporary rocking chair one of these days. Where did you get it?

WOMAN: You can buy them anywhere.

MAN: But this one, where'd you get this one? Where?

WOMAN: Heal's. It's in Tottenham Court Road.

MAN: It's a long way to go for a chair.

WOMAN: They usually have a good selection.

MAN: Mhm. O.K. I'll go to this Heal's and get myself one of these rocking chairs.

WOMAN: You may not be able to get one of these.

MAN: You mean they keep them for special customers?

WOMAN: No, they change their stock.

MAN: Hm. [*Slight pause.*] Well, I can try anyway. They can't kick me out for asking, can they?

[*Pause.*]

WOMAN: Is that what you wanted to ask me about?

MAN: It couldn't be, could it? I mean I didn't even know you *had* a rocking chair till I got in here, did I? It's the first time I've seen in your room. You keep your door closed, don't you? [*Slight pause.*] No, well, you see, I don't want to impose myself on a perfect stranger and start right off asking her advice on this and that.

WOMAN: I'm not a perfect stranger—

MAN: Well, you don't even know my name, do you—?

WOMAN: And anyway I've said I'll be only too glad to help if I can.

MAN: Oh, sure; only you have to think of my point of view. I mean I wasn't talking about you, I was talking about me.

WOMAN: But I don't see anything so terrible about asking my advice on something whether we're strangers or not.

MAN: No, *you* don't; but like I say, I'm talking about *me*. And I'm the one I have to consider. I live here, you know. [*He points to himself.*]

WOMAN [*laughing*]: This is all getting much too serious.

MAN: There aren't any rules, you see. Not for me. I mean, I have to play it by ear, you understand me?

WOMAN: Play what?

MAN: Me. The way I act. There aren't any rules, you see.

[*Slight pause.*]

WOMAN: I'm not sure I know what we're talking about any more.

MAN: Ah, Christ . . . Sorry, do you object to blasphemy?

WOMAN: No, not really. . . .

MAN: Not really means yes?

WOMAN: No, no. . . .

MAN: I'll lay off blasphemy anyway; it gets boring anyway. It's
    just that living alone, I get to blaspheming all the time; it
    comes natural, you know? When you're alone in the room, it
    just goes on all the time. D'you find that? You know what I
    did once. I borrowed this tape-recorder and left it running one
    evening up in the room, and then I played it back. You forget
    about it after a while, forget it's on. You know, this tape was
    full of imprecations—is that the word, or is it invocations?
    Rustle, bang, tap, Oh God, silence, Christ, rustle, tap, God
    Almighty, it was really funny.

WOMAN: I suppose if there's no one else to talk to it's the natural
    thing.

MAN: Yeah. I get you. Yes, that's good. [*He laughs.*] Do you
    believe in Jesus Christ?

WOMAN: Erm. . . .

MAN: No, well, leave that. [*Slight pause.*] You're letting your
    coffee get cold.

WOMAN: I'm sorry, would you like a cup?

MAN: Don't mind me, you just drink it up.

WOMAN: No, really, would you like some coffee?

MAN: Is there any in there?

WOMAN: I'll get you a cup.

[*She gets up, goes out. He remains seated, looking down, apparently
lost in thought. She comes back with a cup and saucer. He remains*

silent, watching her, as she sits down again, puts down the cup and saucer and begins to pour the coffee. The pot is almost empty.]

MAN: I said not to bother about it.

WOMAN: It'll not take a minute to make some more. [*She gets up.*]

MAN: I'm causing you a lot of trouble.

WOMAN [*with a trace of irritation*]: It's no trouble. [*She takes the coffee pot.*] You don't mind instant coffee, do you?

MAN: Is there some other kind?

[*She smiles slightly, and goes out. He ponders again for a moment, looks at her rocking chair, touches it to make it rock slightly, then puts his hand gently palm-down on the upholstered seat of the chair. After a moment he stands up; he has a way of apparently cogitating between his movements—as in his speech—or as though waiting for the next impulse to generate his next action. He stands looking down at the chair, pursing his lips. She can be heard filling the kettle with water, and putting it on the gas. She comes back. He is still standing there, and doesn't look up.*]

WOMAN: D'you want to try it?

MAN: It's your chair.

WOMAN: You're not going to break it, are you?

MAN: You're asking me to sit in it?

WOMAN: For goodness sake, yes.

[*He nods, and sits in the rocking chair. He cogitates solemnly; she sits in his chair.*]

D'you find it comfortable?

MAN: Mhm. . . . [*He looks up suddenly, to catch her eye on him.*] I'll tell you what you're thinking.

WOMAN: All right.

MAN: You're thinking I look like an Uncle Remus.

WOMAN: Hm?

MAN: In the old rocking chair.

WOMAN: I don't understand.

MAN: Let it go. [*Slight pause.*] Yes, its a nice chair. You sit here all the time, hm?

WOMAN: When I'm in the room, yes. In the evenings.

MAN: And who sits in that one?

[*Very slight pause.*]

WOMAN: Friends. People who drop in; like you.

MAN: Only I'm in the rocking chair. [*Slight pause.*] What I was going to say when I blasphemed. . . .

WOMAN: Yes?

MAN: As I said, I have to play things by ear—

WOMAN: What?

MAN: Everything. So now and then I find I've got on the wrong track, and then I just have to backtrack and start again. You know?

WOMAN: Not really. [*Smiling.*]

MAN: Like just now, I mean when I came in here, I shouldn't have said I wanted to ask your advice.

WOMAN: Isn't it true?

MAN: Sure it's true. But you don't blurt out everything that's true just because it's true. Some things you keep till later; some things you just never mention at all.

WOMAN: Yes, but—

[*He waits, but she doesn't continue.*]

MAN: Especially not with a stranger.

WOMAN [*still slightly amused*]: You make communication sound very difficult.

MAN: Communication?

WOMAN: Meeting people.

MAN: Well, for God's sake, I mean, let's not kid ourselves.

[*Slight pause.*]

WOMAN: I mean you make it sound as though—

MAN: I mean don't tell me you find it as easy talking to me as you do sitting by yourself reading that book.

WOMAN: Of course one has to make some effort—

MAN: That's what I'm saying. [*Slight pause.*] D'you see the palms of my hands? Sweat; d'you see? I don't sweat reading books. And I won't ask you to feel my heart, but if you did you'd find it was going bumpity bump like some old donkey-engine. Christ, you can almost hear it.

WOMAN: Why?

MAN: That's the way it goes.

WOMAN: You should meet more people.

MAN: I'd lose too much sweat.

[*He looks intently at her; to cover a growing feeling of embarrassment, she reaches across and picks up her book which was lying open on the table.*]

You want to read again now?

WOMAN [*putting the book down*]: No, of course not.

MAN: I thought this was a gentle hint.

WOMAN: You haven't had your coffee yet.

MAN: Mhm.

WOMAN: When I want you to go I'll say so.

MAN: You do that. [*Slight pause.*] Then why did you pick the book up?

WOMAN: I don't know why I picked the silly book up!

[*He purses his lips.*]

Don't you ever do anything on impulse?

MAN: Sure I do; I do most things on impulse. But not unless I can see some point in it.

WOMAN: That sounds to me rather contradictory.

MAN: Mhm.

WOMAN [*a little angry*]: Well, isn't it? How can you do something on impulse if you deliberate on it?

MAN: I don't get you.

WOMAN: Never mind.

MAN: I mean its all impulses; when you come down to it. You can't make things up out of thin air. You get these impulses to do this and that—and then you work out whether there's any point in doing it. [*Slight pause.*] O.K.?

[*She looks up at him; then nods.*]

That kettle should be boiling.

WOMAN: It'll whistle when it boils.

[*Pause.*]

MAN: What I ought to've said was I'd just come down to say hallo. Then you wouldn't be spending your time bothering over what it is I want to ask you about.

WOMAN: I'm not bothering. [*Slight pause.*] Well all right, if you prefer it that way; you've just come down to say hallo.

MAN: Sure: humour me.

[*Long pause.*]

WOMAN: Would you like a cigarette?

MAN: Thank you, I would.

WOMAN: They're on the table there; can you. . . . ?

[*He picks up the cigarette packet, and offers it to her; she takes one; he then takes one himself, puts the packet down, and feels in his pocket for matches.*]

There's a lighter there somewhere.

[*He finds the lighter, lights her cigarette and his own. There is a pause. The kettle whistles.*]

WOMAN: That's the kettle.

[She gets up and goes out. Left to himself he blows out smoke, cogitates, leans over and picks up her book, looks at the title, closes it; he gets up suddenly, cogitates, puts the book down on the table, cogitates. Then he walks across to the door to the kitchen, and stands this side of it, looking towards where she must be making the coffee. He stands there for a moment, opens his mouth to speak, decides not to, and turns away from the kitchen. He acts, when alone—and sometimes, forgetting himself, in company—like the man who lives inside his own head. He carries his own silence around with him. He might be compared to one of the sea creatures which have means of anchorage but none of propulsion, relying on random currents. When no currents are operating he can be very still; but unlike the sea creature, he knows where he wants to get to—eventually—and is aware of himself, perhaps more aware of himself when no outside forces are acting on him. At such times he has one or two mechanical tricks, mouth movements perhaps, which accentuate both his immobility and his awareness of himself as an article.
He is now by the record player. He lifts the lid, switches it on and off, closes it and looks at the titles of some of the records. She comes back with the coffee. He stands watching her as she takes it to the little table. She pours him a cup.]

WOMAN: Here you are.
MAN: Here I am.

[This kind of difficult exchange, said without humour, is typical of him. She sits down.]

WOMAN: Well. . . .

[He comes over and sits down.]

MAN: Yes, er. . . . May I help myself to sugar?
WOMAN: Yes, of course.

[He does so.]

MAN: Yes, some people like to keep their doors open. Back in the West Indies they don't think of shutting their doors. That's why they get disliked when they come over here. People don't like it. They feel as though it's some kind of effrontery.

WOMAN: It's what?

MAN: An affront. Having to look inside someones else's room; they don't like it.

WOMAN: Why not?

MAN: I can see their point. This old lady on the second floor, she leaves her front door open, you noticed that?

WOMAN: Mrs. Watson.

MAN: You get her cooking smells coming out on the landing. I think she must be boiling up old bones for that dog she keeps in there.

WOMAN: I think she's rather sad really.

MAN: Yeah, sure. She's got a lot of junk in her room; it looks like an old spider's web in there, you know what I mean? You looked in her room?

WOMAN: No. . . .

MAN: You take care not to.

WOMAN: No, it isn't that—

MAN: I don't know what she expects. She expect someone to go into that room, just because the door's open? No one ever will.

WOMAN: I expect she's rather lonely; I've been meaning to call in on her.

MAN: What, give her some old bones to boil up.

WOMAN: I thought I might . . . do something. . . .

MAN: She might just as well shut the door. Keep the smell of her old bones to herself. Be lonely in private.

WOMAN [*a trifle testily*]: One can't help feeling sorry for old people like that—

MAN: That's what I mean. What's the good of making people feel uncomfortable when she never tries to do anything about it?

WOMAN: What do you expect her to do?

MAN: Shut her door.

WOMAN: And die, I suppose.

MAN: Yeah, sure. Just so I don't have to take those stairs two at a time to get past her room.

WOMAN: What would you do in her place?

MAN: How do I know what I'd do? I know what I wouldn't do; I wouldn't make people uncomfortable just for the hell of it.

WOMAN: I'm sure she doesn't do that.

MAN: If I wanted something I'd go out and get it.

WOMAN: And if you couldn't do that?

MAN: I'd keep my door shut.

[*A pause. She spends some time stubbing out her cigarette in the ashtray. He sits immobile.*]

WOMAN: I think it's awful what can happen to old people in London. They spend their lives working and bringing up children. The husband dies, the children go off and get married and move to other places. . . . And nobody bothers about them. . . . I think people really would be relieved if they all did die just as soon as they'd done their jobs in society. . . . I think it's terrible.

MAN: Sure.

WOMAN: They deserve something. They don't ask much.

MAN: They don't ask anything. They just put out their cooking smells.

WOMAN: What do you expect? That's what old people are like! All they've got left is their independence. You can't expect them to come queueing up for relief.

[*Slight pause.*]

MAN: Well, there she is. Her door's open.

[*Pause. She is obviously rather upset.*]

Yeah, there's a whole lot of misfits hanging around London. People you don't wanna know, know what I mean?

[*She picks up the cigarette end and begins to stub it again.*]

You're really taking it out on that cigarette end.

[*She pauses.*]

I mean, what's that cigarette end done to you?

[*He says this without humour. She looks up at him, and gives a kind of smile.*]

I know about this, you see; I used to leave my door open. Not that I boiled bones up there; I just left the door open. Till I got wise to it. All I was doing was causing draughts through the place. Only kids ever go through doors just because they're open.

[*Slight pause.*]

WOMAN: More coffee?
MAN: Thank you.

[*She fills his cup.*]

I closed your book.
WOMAN: What?
MAN: I've lost your place in the book. I picked it up to have a look at it.
WOMAN: It doesn't matter.
MAN: You'll find the place again?
WOMAN: I daresay I shall.
MAN: Is it a good book?
WOMAN: Not really; but it's quite gripping.
MAN: Something to do.
WOMAN: It's a relaxation, I suppose.
MAN: Takes you out of yourself.
WOMAN: I don't read for that reason; I just like reading.
MAN: I mean it's like a way of escaping.

WOMAN: I've got nothing to escape from. [*Slight pause.*]
Don't you read?

[*He shakes his head slowly.*]

Why not?
MAN: Does one need a reason?

[*He drinks; she looks across at him.*]

WOMAN: Are you still playing it by ear?
MAN: I'm sorry, I don't quite get you.
WOMAN: I mean you....
MAN: Mhm?
WOMAN: Nothing, I'm sorry.
MAN: Granted.
WOMAN: You're from the West Indies?
MAN: Not as far as I know.
WOMAN: Oh, I thought you said—
MAN: I might be. I mean it's not impossible.
WOMAN: But you were—you were born in England.
MAN: Sure. Like you, I suppose. . . . I mean, what my ancestors
were up to is none of my business. I've not examined the
family tree.
WOMAN: Oh, I see....
MAN: My mother was English.
WOMAN: Yes?
MAN: Like me.

[*Very slight pause.*]

WOMAN: And your father?
MAN: My father was a bastard. [*Slight pause.*] Yeah, he was
English, too. [*Slight pause.*] So I'm told. And what about you?
[*Slight pause.*] You can offer me a biscuit if you like.
WOMAN: Oh, I'm sorry....

MAN: You don't have to be sorry about everything. I just like biscuits.

WOMAN: Please help yourself.

MAN: I can have one?

WOMAN: I said help yourself.

[*He nods, picks up the biscuit barrel, and offers it to her. She shakes her head. He puts the barrel down next to him on the table and takes a biscuit.*]

MAN: A biscuit barrel. [*Slight Pause.*] That's another thing I must get myself, a biscuit barrel. When I was a kid some other kid invited me back home one day. They had a biscuit barrel on their sideboard. Walnut with silver bands round. This put them straight in the aristocracy.

WOMAN: This was in London?

MAN: Birmingham.

WOMAN: It's strange, you almost seem to have an American accent.

MAN: Oh sure.

WOMAN: You've been to America?

MAN: No; I just picked it up. It's not difficult.

WOMAN: You mean you picked it up on purpose?

MAN: Sure; like you got that biscuit barrel.

[*Slight pause.*]

WOMAN: I got that because I needed it.

MAN: Yeah, sure. But not to put biscuits in. You can put biscuits in anything. You needed a biscuit *barrel*.

WOMAN: But why should anyone need an American accent?

MAN: Why does anyone need anything? It's a cover-up, see? It turns you *into* something. It's like another skin.

WOMAN: Or a mask.

MAN: Sure. Inside, you're O.K. You can fly blind for a while. You've set the course.

WOMAN: But what about the real person inside?
MAN: I'm sorry, I don't follow you.

[*While she is attempting to rephrase the question, he continues.*]

You want to know why I like biscuits?

[*She nods.*]

Me and my kid used to come home from school, you see, midday, and Mum would've left sixpence for us to get something with. Well, you could get a pound of biscuits for sixpence—broken biscuits; so we'd eat those biscuits.
WOMAN: A pound?
MAN: Sure. I'll tell you what we did with the crumbs that were left at the bottom of the bag. We'd tip those crumbs into a saucer, and we'd drop some jam on top, and mix it up with a spoon and eat it. [*Pause.*] Are you going to offer me another biscuit?

[*Slight pause. She laughs.*]

Did I say something funny?
WOMAN: What would you do if I said no?
MAN: No what?
WOMAN: No biscuit.

[*He cogitates for a moment, watching her; he is, as usual, quite serious through all this.*]

MAN: Are you going to offer me another biscuit?
WOMAN: No.
MAN: O.K.

[*She raises her eyebrows, somewhat amused. He watches her.*]

Are you going to offer me another biscuit?
WOMAN: No.

[*He nods. A pause.*]

MAN: Will you offer me a biscuit?

[*Pause. He cogitates, watching her, She shrugs her shoulders, wryly amused.*]

WOMAN: Yes.
MAN: Go on, then.
WOMAN: What?
MAN: Offer me one.
WOMAN: But I've—... Please have a biscuit.
MAN: Thank you.

[*He takes one. She has found it not so funny after all. He eats his biscuit, cogitating; she watches him. He looks up suddenly.*]

I notice you haven't got any Scarlatti.
WOMAN: Hm?
MAN: I was looking at your discs. You like classics.
WOMAN: Oh, I play it now and then, not a great deal.
MAN: I've heard you playing it.
WOMAN: Oh, I'm sorry—
MAN: You're sorry again.
WOMAN: I mean I hope it doesn't disturb you.
MAN: Why should it?
WOMAN: I wondered if I played it too loudly.
MAN: I shouldn't think so. Only the Brahms comes right up into the room. That Brahms has got penetrating power; it comes right through the floorboards.
WOMAN: I'm—....
MAN: It doesn't worry me. You've got no Scarlatti, though.
WOMAN: No, do you like Scarlatti?
MAN: I can take it or leave it, do you?
WOMAN: Yes, I—quite—like it.
MAN: Hang on. [*He gets up.*] I've got a disc by Scarlatti. I'll fetch it.

[*He's off and out before she has time to say anything. Left to herself for a moment, she has time to realise that she is getting into something which, if she had been given the choice, she would have stayed out of; she is, of course, thoroughly broad-minded and liberal; but she hates hurting people's feelings, and doesn't want to be stuck with something which can only be got rid of by doing just that. Also he makes her uneasy, as well he may, since she can't decide whether he's honest or dishonest. Also, and most important, she doesn't consider herself a lonely woman but one who has lived through loneliness and now likes to live alone; and she doesn't much like the possible assumption this relationship implies, that she is grasping at straws— which she knows to be untrue. She frowns, stands up, bites her finger, puts the lid on the biscuit barrel; she looks at her watch. She decides to remain standing. He returns, with the record. He brings it to show her the label.*]

MAN: Sit down, please.

[*She does.*]

Shall I put it on?
WOMAN: Erm. . . .
MAN: You can put it on if you like. It's your record player.
WOMAN: No—no, please put it on.

[*He nods, goes to the record player, puts the record on.*]

Oh, of course. I've heard it, haven't I? I've heard you playing it?

[*He stands facing the record player for a moment, cogitating. Then he turns.*]

MAN: Sure, I play it a lot. It's my record.
WOMAN: Your *only* record?
MAN: Yeah. [*He adjusts the volume.*] I'm not sure it's even mine. If it is, it's mine by—er—acquisition.

WOMAN: How?

MAN: The same way I got this flat, I guess. This bed-sitter with kitchenette. I mean, don't you find it—er—grotesque, that I should have a flat in this house? I mean in this district?

WOMAN: Wh—why?

MAN: And playing Scarlatti and all. Well I'll tell you. This friend of mine had this flat; well, lets say a business acquaintance.

WOMAN: I know, I used to see him now and then. I wondered what happened to him.

MAN: What happened, he's gone abroad for a year; so he sublet it. To me. I think that's funny, don't you, he's gone to South Africa for a year so he sublet the flat to me.

WOMAN: You mean you asked him if he would?

MAN: Let's say it was one of those impulses. He's got a great sense of humour.

[*But he doesn't, of course, laugh.*] And he left this record.

WOMAN: Just one?

MAN: Sure. So what could I do but pick up a record player to play it with?

[*Pause.*] You ever seen the landlord?

WOMAN: Yes, once, when we moved in.

MAN: We?

[*Very slight pause.*]

WOMAN: I was married.

MAN: Mhm.

WOMAN: He seemed quite a nice person.

MAN: The landlord?

WOMAN: Yes.

MAN: Sure. They all are. [*Slight pause.*] One of these days he'll take a look round his property and find it being sublet. He'll say, 'What are you doing here?' and I'll say, 'I'm subletting is that all right?' And he'll tell me to get to hell out, and I'll go. Probably.

WOMAN: He may not.
MAN: Mhm. [*Pause.*] You like this?
WOMAN: Yes.
MAN: You don't have to. I'll switch if off if you want me to.
WOMAN: No please leave it on.

[*Slight pause.*]

MAN: So you could hear me playing this upstairs.
WOMAN: Yes. I didn't mind.
MAN: I'm not apologising. [*He cogitates for a moment.*] What did you think when you heard it?
WOMAN: Of the music?
MAN: No. I mean here's some music coming into your private room uninvited. You know someone's at the other end, responsible for it.
WOMAN: I didn't realise it was you; I mean I didn't connect it with you.
MAN: That's understandable.
WOMAN: It was just music.
MAN: You didn't feel outraged?
WOMAN: Of course not. Did you, when you heard the Brahms?
MAN: Who am I to feel outraged? [*Pause.*] Do you have a visitor this evening?

[*Slight giveaway pause.*]

WOMAN: Well—yes, as a matter of fact. I think someone is coming later. [*She looks at her watch.*]
MAN: Mhm. [*He stops the music.*]
WOMAN: What was it you wanted to ask me?

[*He looks at her.*]

You said you wanted some advice.
MAN: Yes, now . . . if you ring these people up, tell them not to come this evening . . . then you can ask me to go to bed with you.

[*Long pause.*]

WOMAN: Would you mind getting out?
MAN: You're asking me to go?
WOMAN: I'm telling you to go.

[*Pause. He nods.*]

MAN: O.K. [*He turns and begins to go.*]
     So I'm coloured. [*He opens the door.*]
WOMAN: How dare you!

[*He stops in the doorway and looks back at her.*]

Get out! Please get out!

[*He goes, closing the door softly behind him. She stands stiffly for a moment, then puts her hands to her face, breathing deeply. While she stands there, there is a knock at the door. She takes a step or two back, watching the door. The knock is repeated. A pause.*]

Who is it?

[*He speaks from behind the closed door.*]

MAN: I forgot something.

[*Slight pause. She opens the door. He enters.*]

I forgot to take my disc. My Scarlatti.

[*She nods. He goes to the record player and takes the record. He pauses very slightly at the door, and goes out again, closing the door gently behind him. After he has gone she remains still for a moment, then begins to cry. She wanders back to her chair—the rocking chair —still crying, and sits down, crying as one suffering from mild shock. She gradually subsides, her head still bent in her hands; she occasionally heaves with a sob, like a child. Above, from his room, is heard the Scarlatti. He must be playing it quite loudly. Her sobs stop for a moment; she is motionless in the chair, her face hidden;*]

then she begins shaking again; but when she raises her face it is seen that she is laughing, giggling, uncontrollably. She gets up, still giggling, puts the coffee things on the tray and takes it into the kitchen, where she is heard unloading it and washing up. Meanwhile the music upstairs continues for a while, then stops suddenly. So do the noises from the kitchen, as though she was listening. There is a pause; she appears at the kitchen door, a cloth in her hands, and waits, watching the other door. There is a knock at the door. She raises her eyebrows—her face is almost cynical—and waits. The knock is repeated. She waits a moment, then goes back into the kitchen, without haste. There is a long pause, and the knock is repeated. A pause, then she returns to the room, unhurriedly, looks round quickly, and sits down in her rocking chair with the book. She lights a cigarette, and apparently reads. The knock is repeated. A slight pause; she looks up.]

WOMAN: Come in.

[*The door opens, and he stands just inside the rooms, still with his hand on the handle, as at his first entrance.*]

Please close the door.

MAN: Which side of it do you want me to be on?

WOMAN: I've asked you to come in.

[*He closes the door, as in his first entrance.*]

What is it you want?

MAN: What is it you want?

WOMAN: You knocked—

MAN: You asked me to come in. . . . You knew it was me out there. Here I am.

WOMAN: I don't want people knocking on my door all the evening, that's all. If you have something more to say to me, say it, and then you can go. [*Pause.*] What is it you want?

MAN: You don't have to be afraid of me, you know.

WOMAN: Don't be ridiculous, I'm not afraid of you; I can look after myself.

MAN: Sure you can. You're the right colour.

WOMAN: I just want you to say whatever else it is you want to say, get your grievances off your chest, so that I shan't be bothered with you again.

[*He nods. Slight pause.*]

MAN: You don't have to be bothered with me. Just tell me to go and I'll go.

WOMAN: And a minute later you'll be back knocking again.

MAN: I wouldn't do that.

WOMAN: You've already done it once.

MAN: Sure, that's why I wouldn't do it again. That'd be a legal offence. What is it, committing a nuisance, isn't that it? I can't afford to commit any offences. All you'd have to do is ring the police station, say 'Look, I'm being pestered here by this coloured gentleman who shouldn't be here at all anyway, he's only subletting;' they'd be round like a shot. They'll believe you. Come to that, you could do it now. Ring up and tell them I've been knocking at your door all evening and won't go away. If you like you could say I tried to rape you; that'd bring them round here *really* fast. Then you can ring the landlord, this pleasant fellow, do you have his number? Tell him I'm living here. He'll be here in the morning. You see, like I say, you don't have to worry.

WOMAN: What kind of a person do you think I am?

MAN: Look, I don't know you, do I? I don't even know your name. I don't know what kind of a person you are. I'm just making a few suggestions, to put your mind at rest.

[*Slight pause.*]

WOMAN: Very well. I'm white, I don't dislike Negroes, I think they have a—a raw deal, I dislike you and I want to be left alone. Is that enough?

MAN: Mhm. Sure. I mean you're what they call a liberal, aren't you? You're liberal minded; old women, Negroes. . . . Yeah, tell me—who are these Negros you don't dislike? Maybe I know one or two of them. . . . [*Pause.*] You want me to go, you just tell me to go.

WOMAN: And you won't be back.

MAN: Tell me to go and I'll go; I won't be back today.

WOMAN: So I'm to expect you at breakfast time?

MAN: I don't know about that. I get up pretty late some mornings. What time do you eat breakfast? [*Pause.*] No, well, you see, I don't want to make any promises one way or the other. I mean, we're neighbours, isn't that so? One over the other, is that neighbours, or do they have to be side by side? I mean, if I find I've got any more, you know, if I want to ask your advice again on some matter, I might give a neighbourly knock one day, one morning or evening—

WOMAN: I'd better tell you that if you do annoy me any further I shall call the police immediately.

MAN: Sure; that's what I was saying.

[*Slight pause.*]

WOMAN: And now please go.

MAN: O.K. [*Slight pause.*] Yeah. Only we'd better just get it straight, hadn't we? I mean, can we get it straight first?

WOMAN: What?

MAN: What I'm allowed to do. I want to be careful, I mean in my position I have to be careful not to overstep the mark. So if you just tell me where the mark is I'll take care not to over-step it. I don't want to get back to my room one day and find the police there waiting for me, or the landlord, this pleasant chap. So you just tell me the rules of the game. Knocking on your door for instance, now I take it I'm not to knock on your door any more. That's for ever, is it? I mean, for instance, if I wake up one night and the house is on fire, and I knock on your door, will you call the police in? I want to cover myself, you see? Not that I can ever cover myself, because you're the one they'll believe, but it'll help put my mind at rest if there's some kind of, er, rule of thumb, you know? All these people you liberals don't dislike, we're crazy about rules of thumb. We're kind of quaint that way. We don't like getting our bottoms kicked, it's an idiosyncrasy, so we get ourselves these rules of thumb. We still get kicked anyway, that goes without saying, but that way we can blame ourselves for it instead of whoever's doing the kicking.

WOMAN: Look, you know exactly what I—

MAN: Not exactly; that's the point I'm trying to make, you see, we never know exactly. Now, as to passing you on the stairs, which as you say is near enough. I can't see how I can avoid passing you on the stairs now and then, unless we work out some kind of timetable, who's to be on the stairs when, and you wouldn't like that, it'd interfere with your freedom. And I can't get out through the window, not on the fourth floor, so we're stuck with it unless you like to ring the landlord, this good chap, and then you won't see me on the stairs any more. Failing that, am I to nod to you or not? I don't want to overstep the mark, but I don't want you thinking I'm being insolent or anything like that by ignoring you. You see my point?

WOMAN: Go away, please, go away.

MAN: Sure, sure, just one last point. About my Scarlatti.

WOMAN: What about it? You've got it, haven't you?

MAN: Sure, only the point is, you see, am I to be allowed to play it?

WOMAN: You can do as you like as long as you keep out of my way.

MAN: Mhm. Only it's not that simple, is it? I mean, as you say, when I play my Scarlatti it doesn't stay in my room, it comes down into your room as well. I suppose in a way you could call it trespassing; I don't imagine you want my Scarlatti wandering around your room uninvited. I mean, your Brahms, that's all right, after all I'm not supposed to be here, I'm only subletting.

WOMAN: You can play your record as much as you like, it doesn't worry me.

MAN: Mhm.

WOMAN: If you want to be treated like a child I'll treat you like one.

MAN: That's right, you do that. That's what I want. You just go ahead and treat me like a child, it'll make me feel at home. We're all just great simple children, everyone knows that.

WOMAN: Very well. Now will you go?

MAN: Don't ask me, tell me. I mean you ask a kid to do things he *wants* to do; if there's something he doesn't want to do, you have to *tell* him.

WOMAN: Go then. Go. Clear out.

[*He nods.*]

MAN: That's it. We understand that. Authority; that's where we feel at home.

[*He puts his hand on the door handle, and cogitates for a moment.*]

Er.... That old lady, old Mrs ... old Mrs Watson ... If you've got any old bones in the kitchen, you might take them down there some time for her to boil up. She'd appreciate that! I mean she'd feel grateful, you know? You don't have to go in there ... Just leave them outside the door ...

[*He opens the door, looks at her as he is about to go out. She is almost uncontrollably angry.*]

And, er, thank you for your help. I'll tell my friends ...

2—NAOP

WOMAN: Wait! How dare you . . . ? How dare you talk to me like that?

[*He shrugs his shoulders, still standing in the doorway. A slight pause.*]

MAN: You want me to go or not?

WOMAN: I want you to get something straight first.

MAN: Mhm. You want the door open or closed then? I mean, that dear old lady downstairs, she'll be listening in with her door open . . .

[*She walks up to him, as though she is going to strike him, and pushes the door shut with a slam. There is a pause; she looks at him with blazing eyes; he looks back with his usual lack of expression, though underneath it there is the knowledge that he has worked things so that he is still in the room. She is perhaps also aware of this as a sort of triumph on his part; to regain her superior position, and also to weigh her words, she turns her back on him and walks away, across to the chairs, where she stands with one hand on the back of the rocking chair, still facing away from him. He waits. She turns.*]

WOMAN: What kind of chip it is you carry on your shoulder is none of my business; I'm just not interested. I only want to make it quite clear that I've treated you only as I would have treated anyone who came in here and made the—kind of suggestion you made. I think you've behaved in a—disgusting way, and the most despicable thing of all is to—try to excuse yourself, try to put the blame on me by making oblique remarks about your colour. I don't give a damn what colour you are. But I tell you this much; if you'd been a white man and come in here and asked me a thing like that, I'd not have waited so long before kicking you out, and you'd have had your face smacked into the bargain . . . As it was, I did my best to be friendly to you . . . I did my best . . . [*Tears have come into her eyes again. She wipes them away with the handkerchief. Her voice drops.*] Oh, leave me alone. Go away, get out of my sight. I think you're disgusting.

[*Pause. He looks down at his feet. She shakes her head slowly. Slight pause.*]

MAN: You think I've let the side down.

[*She looks across at him.*]

WOMAN: I don't know what you mean.

MAN: I mean, as you say, if I'd been what you call a white man you'd have just slapped my face and kicked me out, and that would've been that.

WOMAN: I don't want to argue any longer. As far as I'm concerned that's that anyway.

MAN: No, but it isn't, you see. Don't worry, I don't mean I'm going to pester you.

WOMAN: Then what do you mean?

MAN: [*quietly and without insolence*]: Well, I mean, if it had been a white man it wouldn't have worried you so much because men are like that, isn't that so? I mean, men are bastards. Well, you've been married, you know that. But, er, coloured people, you expect them to be different.

WOMAN: I've told you this has nothing to do with colour.

MAN: Oh, sure, I understand that. I acted like a bastard, there's no denying that. Well, look what happens; here are people like you, I mean liberal people, progressives, you know, going out of their way to be nice to us people and try to understand us and make allowances for us and what happens? As soon as you really do *meet* one he does a thing like this. I don't suppose you've met many coloured people, have you?

[*She says nothing.*]

I mean not recently.

WOMAN: What are you trying to say?

MAN: Oh, I'm not excusing myself. Don't get me wrong. I'm not saying we just have to act this way because of the way we're treated—

WOMAN: I think that's absolutely—

MAN: Yeah, absolutely, that's true. There's no excuse for me to come in here and after you've tried to be extra nice and understanding to me because I'm coloured, to go and say a thing like that thing I said.

[*Pause.*]

WOMAN: Are you trying to apologise?

[*Pause. He cogitates.*]

MAN: I suppose that's what I am doing . . . Yes, I'm saying I'm sorry for saying that. [*Pause.*] Asking you off the cuff like that to go to bed with a coloured person . . .

WOMAN: Why do you keep bringing that up! I tell you it's nothing to me! [*Pause.*] I—look, you've apologised; at least I think you've apologised; I don't really know what you're trying to get at; I accept your apology; I'm sorry too; I'm sorry it ever happened; perhaps I was—too friendly or something; now can we—forget the whole thing and leave it at that?

MAN: Mhm. OK. Though I'd, er, just like to say this one thing. If I may.

[*Slight pause.*]

WOMAN: Yes.

MAN: Oh, but I've been forgetting, your, er, your visitor.

WOMAN: Hm?

MAN: This person you're expecting this evening. I don't want to make you late; I mean you'll want to get ready, and anyway you won't want him coming and finding me here.

WOMAN: Why not?

[*He shrugs his shoulders.*]

MAN: Now don't misunderstand me; I know *you* don't mind; only some people might, I mean there *are* people like that about, aren't there?

WOMAN: He's a friend of mine.

[*Slight pause.*]

MAN: Sure, yes.

WOMAN: You really have an inferiority complex, don't you?

MAN: Yes. [*Slight pause.*] I suppose it's like that joke, you know? Where this psychiatrist says to the patient, 'I've at last discovered what's wrong with you. You really are inferior.'

[*He laughs. She shakes her head—part negation—part bewilderment.*]

Yes, just this one er, thing I wanted to say; before I go; so you can get ready for your visitor . . . [*Slight pause.*] All I wanted to say was this . . . [*Pause, while he apparently chooses his words*] Just because I came in here and acted, er . . . acted out of turn, I shouldn't like to think this is going to affect your attitude towards us in general.

WOMAN: Towards . . .

MAN: Us.

WOMAN: Why on earth should it?

MAN: Why shouldn't it? I mean—

WOMAN: I don't have any *attitude*. I thought I'd make that clear.

MAN: Well, yes, in that case I see, in that case what I did couldn't make any difference to my—let's say my brothers. If you don't have any attitude. I just thought you did have.

WOMAN: Then you thought wrong.

MAN: Sure, that's my inferiority complex out again. Only I thought you said you treated coloured people different from the others—

WOMAN: I said no such thing—

MAN: Like you would've—slapped my face if I'd been white.

[*Slight pause.*]

WOMAN: Well *of course* I—

MAN: You try to make allowances.

WOMAN: Perhaps I *should* have slapped your face, is that what you wanted! Am I supposed to apologise now for not slapping your face!

MAN: No, look, I think you're misunderstanding me. Good Lord, who am I to tell *you* how to behave?

WOMAN: For God's sake, what's the matter with you? I try to be nice to people, I try to be kind, you come in here and you're obviously lonely and I—I try to *redress the balance* a little! That's all! Do you think I need you to tell me the world isn't quite fair to, to—coloured people? It's not my fault, you know. There's nothing I can do about it! All I can do is try and— swing the balance a little in the other direction, to go out of my way to be nicer and—more understanding than I usually would. [*Slight pause.*] Very well, in future I'll treat everyone the same, if that's what you want; I'll slap their faces as soon as they do anything I don't like!

[*Pause.*]

MAN: But you don't have any attitude towards coloured people—

WOMAN: Well if that's what you mean by attitude—

MAN: That's all I meant.

[*Slight pause.*]

WOMAN: All right, my attitude towards coloured people is different from my attitude towards white people. I'm very sorry.

MAN: You don't have to be sorry.

WOMAN: Then why do you make snide remarks about it?

MAN: I didn't make any snide remarks. All I said was you had an attitude, and you said you hadn't, that's all. I didn't ask you to *change* your attitude, did I? What I said was, I hoped what I did *wouldn't* change your attitude.

[*She sighs, and puts her hand over her eyes; turns away from him and goes to the table; picks up the cigarettes, but at present merely plays with the packet. A long pause.*]

WOMAN: What do you want? [*Pause.*] What is it you want? What do you want me to say? What do you want me to do?

[*Slight pause.*]

MAN: There was only that one thing . . . Just to be sure you won't think differently just because of my behaviour.

WOMAN: You put my mentality pretty low, don't you, to think I'd do that?

MAN: No, I don't, really. I think you're a very intelligent person, if I may say so.

[*She half smiles. A pause.*]

WOMAN: Do you want a cigarette?

MAN: No, thank you.

[*She has one herself. He walks across to the table, picks up the lighter and lights it for her.*]

WOMAN: Thank you. [*Slight pause.*] As far as I'm concerned people are individuals. I don't make up general rules, I thought I'd explained that.

MAN: Yes, only you do treat us people better than you do the white ones, so I suppose you think we deserve it. Or need it. I'd just hate to think you were going to change your mind about that and decide you ought to treat us *worse* than the whites. After all, you must have made up the rule in the first place, there's no reason why you shouldn't change it now you've actually *met* a Negro.

WOMAN: Do you think I haven't met Negroes before?

MAN: Well, I don't know. I mean, I expect I'm the first to set foot in this room for instance. And I don't imagine you've ever had one to dinner, say—

WOMAN: If I knew any Negroes I would!

MAN: Sure, that's what I'm saying. This visitor, is he a Negro?

WOMAN: Look—Look, I'm feeling a little tired . . . As far as I'm concerned I don't bear any grudge about what happened; I'm willing to forget it ever did happen. And, of course, any evening you feel like dropping in—for a few minutes I'll be delighted to see you. But now I really have got some things I must do and—

MAN: And the visitor.

WOMAN: Yes, and the visitor.

MAN: Mhm. [*He nods. There is a pause.*] There's no visitor.

WOMAN: Hm?

MAN: There isn't any visitor. Is there? There isn't any bloody visitor.

WOMAN: Oh God . . .

MAN: Is there? Is there?

WOMAN: No! ! !

MAN: They why the hell did you say there was? Don't you have enough superiority already, couldn't you just say, look, I've had enough of you, now I want you to go, do you have to lie as well?

WOMAN [*breaking into this*]: I don't have to give an account of myself to you!

MAN: Don't you! You're the superior being, isn't that just what you *do* have to do! ?

WOMAN: All right, I was lying. There's no visitor. And now I've had enough of you, so get out! Get out, before I call the police!

MAN: Call them, then! Call the bloody police.

[*He takes the telephone, dials 999 and thrusts the stand into one of her hands and the handset into the other.*]

Go on, go on!

[*She looks at the telephone as though dazed.*]

What's the matter, can't you think of a complaint? Can't you make up any more lies? Here, I'll help you! [*At the record player, he takes a record at random and reads out the label.*] J S Bach.

[*He takes out a flick-knife and scores it viciously across. She looks round, her face expressionless. His face is now the one which has begun to show expression.*]

Here's another. Mozart [*He scores it across*] Get the police, then, get them. How many more do you need?

WOMAN: Please don't . . . please, don't . . .

[*He stands by the records, staring at her, panting. She puts the telephone down, with the handset on. There is a pause; she sits down, quietly, very straight and tense, not looking at him. He breathes out, noisily, as though to release tension, and relaxes somewhat. There is a long pause, while they both remain motionless. Then he goes to the cigarettes, and takes one, There is nothing bold in this, it is done without thought. He lights it. They are not looking at each other.*]

I don't even know your name . . . [*She says this without looking at him, hardly at all. Pause.*] I don't even know your name . . .

[*She says it again with a whimper, and is crying again.*]

MAN: What the hell are you crying about? If you've got something to cry about, you tell me what it is.

[*A pause.*]

WOMAN: What is it you want?

[*He says nothing, but stands looking at the back of his hand.*]

You want to accuse me of something? Accuse me, then, come out into the open with it. What have I really done to you? What?

MAN: You think if you know my name it'll make everything OK?

WOMAN: Is it the way I nodded to you on the stairs? Didn't I nod hard enough, or shouldn't I have nodded at all? What am I supposed to *do*?

MAN: It's Rastus. I'm not really English, you've guessed that already. I was born in a log cabin on the banks of the Mississippi. Yas *sah*. Ah remember mah deah ole mammy saying to me. Rastus, she say, now don't you never fergit to be a good li'l piccaninny an do as the Massa tells you—

WOMAN [*breaking in*]: For God's sake, can I help it if you're coloured?

[*Slight pause.*]

MAN: No ma'am. [*Slight pause.*] You know what I did once when I was a kid? I was alone in the house, everyone else was out. So I took some of this stuff you use for scouring out the bath—not that we had any bath, I mean, you can't have everything, can you? I thought to myself, if it gets stains off baths and lavatory bowls like it says on the packet, it'll get this off sure enough. So I went to work on the back of my hand with this stuff and some hot water and a scrubbing brush. Yas, sah . . . No, you're quite right. You can't help it if I'm coloured. You're liberal, I know that. If you could make me white, you'd make me white, Yas, sah. . . .

WOMAN: What do you want me to *do*? [*Pause.*] Go to bed with you because you're coloured?

[*Pause.*]

MAN: Well, now, that'd be kinky, wouldn't it? I wouldn't expect you to do a thing like that. On the other hand, now if it was in *spite* of my being coloured, that's a Christian thing to do, isn't that right? Like kissing the leper.

[*Pause.*]

WOMAN: Is that the way you like to think of yourself?
MAN: Is there some other way?

[*Pause.*]

WOMAN: Why don't you see a psychiatrist?
MAN: Sure. You know any good coloured ones? [*Slight pause.*] Not that that makes any difference to you.
WOMAN: What do you mean?
MAN: I mean you're one of those liberals, aren't you? If someone's got a bit of a kink somewhere, you don't condemn them because of that, do you, any more than you condemn coloured people for being coloured? Good God, no, liberals aren't like that. You make allowances, isn't that so, you try to be extra kind to them because it's not really their fault, I mean let's be progressive. You try to be extra kind and understanding to them and at the same time you treat them just exactly the same as you'd treat anyone else, isn't that so?

[*She says nothing.*]

Isn't that so?
WOMAN: My God, you're just playing on it, aren't you?
MAN: Yeah, that's an extra kink I got, playing on my kink. That makes it a double kink. Plus I'm coloured. If only I could wet my bed at nights I'd have a full house, a real winning hand. You liberals'd be falling over backwards. [*Slight pause.*] You want to blame me for something? You want to blame me for being neurotic? [*Slight pause.*] OK then. You see, ma'am, what you've got is a real *case* on your hands; but you're liberal minded, you can cope with that. Isn't that so? Or doesn't your liberalism stretch quite that far?

WOMAN: Please don't try to take advantage of me—

MAN: Oh, I get it. You don't want to be taken advantage of. Like you'll be progressive till it kills you, just so long as nobody takes advantage of you. Yeah, sure; and when you pass a blind man in the street with his cap out, what do you do? You ask to see his doctor's certificate and bank account.

WOMAN: You're twisting everything I say!—

MAN: Sure I am, that's the way I am. I twist. I'm twisted. Like I say, you've got a real solid case on your hands. Well, OK, you're the sane one, you're the balanced one, you're the white one, you're the *liberal*—humour me! Be kind to me! Understand me ! !

[*His voice breaks on this, he covers his face in hands and sobs, shortly; he soon stops, but keeps his face covered. She suddenly yells at him.*]

WOMAN: Why don't you get out of my life?

[*A slight pause. He breathes out noisily as before, takes his hands away, and they look at each other. He sits down. A pause.*]

What am I going to do . . . ?

[*Slight pause.*]

MAN: Well now . . . I guess we're both in the same boat; we're at evens.

[*She looks at him, waiting for the explanation.*]

You've run out of liberalism, and I've run out of impulses.

WOMAN: Run out? Or aren't they necessary any more . . . ? Of course, this is what you were trying to do, isn't it?

[*He says nothing.*]

Strip Jack naked, isn't that it? Only I mustn't say you were *trying* to do it. It's all done by impulses, isn't it? [*Slight pause.*]

Isn't there any point at which you begin to be responsible for yourself?

MAN: You ... tell ... me.

[*Slight pause.*]

WOMAN: You really run deep, don't you?

MAN: My kind do ...

WOMAN: Not your kind; you. You can drop that line now. As you say, I've run out of liberalism, I don't generalise any more ... And now we're at evens ... Or have you won?

[*There is a slight pause, as they watch one another.*]

MAN: I guess getting even is winning.

[*Slight pause.*]

WOMAN: So what now? The presentation of the trophy? [*Pause.*] Give me another cigarette, please.

MAN: You smoke too much.

WOMAN: Please give me a cigarette.

[*He takes a single cigarette out of the packet and offers it to her. She hesitates for a moment, then takes it. Her face is hard. They look at one another for a moment. She give it back to him and speaks very curtly.*]

Light it for me.

[*He puts it in his mouth, lights it and hands it to her. He watches her as she takes a draw at it.*]

How right you are. I've nothing to cry about. You've done nothing to me. There's nothing you can do.

[*He is puzzled. She stands up, looks down at him, then goes to the record player.*]

Let's have some music, shall we?

[*She looks through the records, selects one, puts it on, low volume. Brahms. She comes back to the chairs, and stubs her cigarette carefully out in the ashtray, watching him. She waits a moment, then switches off the table lamp. A faint light is still left in the room. She goes across to the divan and sits on it. She takes off her shoes, and drops them on the floor one by one. The noise of their fall is heard above the music. She curls her legs under her on the divan. A pause.*]

Well . . . ? Or do you want it with the light on . . . ?

[*Slight pause. He stands up, goes across to the divan and puts his arms round her; she falls back on to the divan. There is a long, long pause. Nothing is heard but the sound of the music; the figures on the bed are quite still. He suddenly cries out, as though he has been physically hurt.*]

MAN: Oh God!!!

[*He falls to his knees, his head buried in bed; she stands up.*]

WOMAN: What's the matter?

[*He makes no response. She goes to the chairs.*]

MAN: Don't turn the light on!

[*She stops, and looks back at him. He raises his head, gets up and stands with his back to her. She waits a moment then crosses to the record player, and switches it off. She remains standing there. He turns, but so that his face is always away from her, goes to the chairs, and sits down, head bowed, one hand covering his face. A pause. She goes to the table lamp and turns it on. The top of her dress is unbuttoned; she buttons it up. Then she takes his wrist and pulls it away from his face, so that the light shines on it. He looks up at her. Then he begins to laugh. At first it seems to be a laugh of triumph, but then it is noticeable that there is something of hysteria about it.*]

It's great, isn't it . . . That when it finally comes down to it— I'm incapable!

[*She continues to look at him.*]

WOMAN: You want to blame me for that too?

[*A pause.*]

MAN: That's what we get by on, you know? That myth. That's all they allow us . . . I mean we haven't got any *culture* or anything like that. [*Pause.*] All we've got is this great . . . *Myth* . . . *Myth.*

[*Pause.*]

WOMAN: You want to try it again? [*Long pause.*] Do you . . . ? [*Pause.*] It's nothing . . . It happens . . . For goodness sake, don't you know that? [*Pause.*] Well, say something.

MAN: What am I supposed to say? Thank you?

WOMAN: You can say what you damned well like: just don't sit there accusing me!

MAN: I'm not accusing you—

WOMAN: No? Then what? What are you sitting there for? What more do you expect of me? [*Pause.*] What am I supposed to do now?

[*He shakes his head slowly. Pause.*]

Then why don't you go . . . ?

[*He gets up. Pause.*]

For God's sake—go away, and leave me alone . . .

[*He goes to the door, pauses at the door.*]

MAN: I'd be OK in my room . . . If you'd come up . . . to my room . . . I'd be OK . . .

WOMAN: Please get out.

[*He doesn't move.*]

Will you please go, will you please go? Will you please go!?

[*He goes out, closing the door gently behind him. When he has gone, she has a sudden burst of crying, and stands irresolutely, her back to the audience. After a while she walks to the table, and picks up the cigarettes, almost unconsciously. From upstairs comes the sound of the Scarlatti. She begins to cry again. Then she goes to the record player, and puts on the Brahms. The Scarlatti can still be heard over it. She puts the volume full up, drowning the Scarlatti. She stands there for a while, crying, then sweeps the arm off the record. The Scarlatti is still playing. She walks slowly to the door, still crying, and goes out.*]

TRIO

First performance by the Traverse Theatre Company, Edinburgh, Autumn 1967

CHARACTERS
in order of appearance

VIOLIN

VIOLA

CELLO

TRIO

[*The stage is set for a string trio. After a moment the members of the trio enter:* VIOLIN, *male;* VIOLA, *female;* CELLO, *male. Applause as they sit down. The* VIOLIN *rises again and holds up his hand for silence.*]

VIOLIN: Your Holiness . . . Your Imperial Majesty . . . Mr President, my Lords, Alderman and Burghers, Ladies and Gentlemen . . . I am a Musician, not a speechmaker. Our music shall speak for us. Culture knows no frontiers, music knows no distinction of race, creed or colour. Let me say but this; we have shed each other's blood. We have destroyed each other's cities. We have slain each other's kin. We were mad. It is forgotten. We are brothers all.

[*He sits down. Great applause.* VIOLA *and* CELLO *applaud back, beaming.*
VIOLIN *raises his violin, looks questioningly round at* CELLO, *who looks questioningly round at* VIOLA.
VIOLA *nods to* CELLO: CELLO *nods to* VIOLIN. VIOLIN *raises his bow. An aircraft passes overhead.*
VIOLIN *lowers his bow and waits.* CELLO *points his bow like a rifle at the sky and pulls the trigger, grinning.* VIOLA *sniggers behind her hand.* VIOLIN *looks round, and turns back to the audience, grinning, and waits. The aircraft recedes into the distance.*
VIOLIN *looks questioningly round at* CELLO, *who looks questioningly round at* VIOLA. VIOLA *nods to* CELLO, CELLO *nods to* VIOLIN. VIOLIN *raises his bow.*
They begin to play.
After a few bars CELLO *shakes his head, the music falters, and stops. A tiny fly is buzzing about* CELLO's *head, its voice just audible.*
VIOLIN *looks round at* CELLO. CELLO *grimaces, shrugs, rubs his nose, and waves his bow in the air.*

VIOLA *frowns, a little embarrassed.*
VIOLIN *waits.* CELLO *looks at* VIOLIN, *and nods. They prepare to play. The music starts. It goes on for a little, then* CELLO *begins to shake his head from side to side. The music swoops a little and falters, but continues.* VIOLA *glances at* CELLO. *The sound of a fly is again heard, but a rather bigger one. It recedes, but then again swoops:* CELLO *shakes his head again, then waves his bow in the air and finally slaps his face. Music of course, stops.* CELLO *looks round his seat, finds the fly and treads on it. Meanwhile* VIOLA *sits stiffly, not looking at him, with compressed lips.*
VIOLIN *glares at him,* CELLO *looks up, looks at* VIOLIN, *shrugs his shoulders.* VIOLIN *glares.*
CELLO *puts his bow at the ready, and nods.* VIOLIN *glares at the audience and prepares to play. They begin.*
Immediately an immense fly is heard. CELLO *tries to keep his eyes on it while playing. The fly dives,* VIOLIN, CELLO *and* VIOLA *duck in turn. The fly returns, and they duck again in reverse order. Music stops, and* VIOLIN *jumps up and waves his arms and bow around wildly.*]

VIOLIN: Merde! Merde! Merde!!

[*The fly goes,* CELLO *shrugs,* VIOLIN *marches off stage, and is heard and partly seen in heated altercation. Meanwhile* VIOLA's *face crumbles, and she bursts into tears.* CELLO *stands up and bends over her to comfort her, steadying his cello meanwhile. He gives her his handkerchief.*]

VIOLA: I said we shouldn't have come, didn't I say so?

[*He pats her hand, then kisses it. She looks into his eyes.* VIOLIN *returns with a fly-spray. He stands and looks round with it ready. He glares at the audience.*]

VIOLIN: In my country it would not be considered funny.

[*He lets off a couple of bursts at the ceiling and sits down.*]

VIOLA: They're not like us!

[CELLO *pats her hand.*]

CELLO: Ssh, ssh.

> VIOLIN *glares at them,* CELLO *sits down and prepares to play.* VIOLA, *sniffing, prepares to play. She sniffs again.* VIOLIN *glares at her. Glares at the audience raises his bow, and puts his fly spray to his chin. Realises his mistake, throws down the spray and marches off stage, returning with his* VIOLIN. *All prepare to play. A droning is heard in the distance. The trio freezes. It comes nearer, and then roars down to make a number of attacks.*
> VIOLIN *throws down his violin, picks up the fly-spray and leaps furiously about letting it off in all directions. Meanwhile* CELLO *gallantly protects* VIOLA. *The attacker dives again.* VIOLIN *ducks,* VIOLA *screams and clutches her arm.*]

CELLO: They've hit her! Murderers!
VIOLIN: Swine!

[*He fires his spray-gun. The attacker crashes.*]

CELLO: A defenceless woman!
VIOLIN: We consider this an act of deliberate provocation!
VIOLA: I said we shouldn't have come. Savages, savages!
CELLO: We offer you the hand of friendship—
VIOLIN: It's no use talking to them. They'll laugh at you.
VIOLA: Stab you in the back—
VIOLIN: Savages!
VIOLA: To think my sister married one of them!

[CELLO *draws away from her.*]

CELLO: You never told me that.
VIOLA: She had to . . .

[*She sobs.*]

VIOLIN: The swine stop at nothing.

CELLO: Well, that's that. Let's go.

VIOLIN: Are you mad?

CELLO: You don't want us to stay?

VIOLIN: You think we should run away?

CELLO: What?

VIOLIN: Our tails between our legs?

CELLO: I wasn't thinking about tails.

VIOLIN: Then you should.

CELLO: I'm an artiste. I'm not concerned with tails.

VIOLIN: You're an artiste second. First, you are a son of your Motherland, or Fatherland.

CELLO: Yes, that goes without saying, but—

VIOLIN: What do you think they want?

CELLO: Music?

VIOLIN: Nonsense. Do you think they want music? I knew all along they didn't want music, they're not interested in music.

CELLO: Then what are we doing here?

VIOLIN: We were invited. We had to come. A matter of prestige.

CELLO: But why did they invite us?

VIOLIN: To humiliate us.

CELLO: Us?

VIOLIN: Our Fatherland or Motherland. They want us to run off, our tails between our legs. Then they'll laugh at us.

CELLO: The curs.

VIOLIN: So much for *their* Fatherland or Motherland, they'll say, compared to *our* Fatherland or Motherland. That's why they're sending these things over.

CELLO: But we can't play under these conditions.

VIOLIN: You want us to confess we're beaten? Is that the spirit that wins wars?

CELLO: We aren't at war.

VIOLIN: Defeatist, defeatist!

CELLO: I'm a musician—

VIOLIN: Remember the Battle of Tonkerman!

CELLO: We lost the Battle of Tonkerman!

VIOLIN: The Battle of Balawi, then.

VIOLA: We lost the—

VIOLIN: Am I the leader of this trio or not?! Remember whichever damned battle you like. It makes no difference. We acquitted ourselves well. We fought to the last conscript. We destroyed all the villages. We taught them a lesson.

CELLO: Who?

VIOLIN: Everybody.

[*Pause.*]

CELLO: So what do you suggest?

VIOLIN: A change of programme. Strategy, my friend. A duo for viola and cello.

CELLO: What about you?

VIOLIN: I shall stand guard. To be followed by a duo for viola and violin while you stand guard, to be followed by a duo for violin and cello while she stands guard.

VIOLA: I'm a non-combatant.

VIOLIN: In war there's no such thing.

VIOLA: And I'm wounded.

VIOLIN: So?

VIOLA: I can't play.

VIOLIN: Are you a wog?

VIOLA: How dare you.

VIOLIN: Or a chink? Or a wop or a limey or a yank or a hun or a frog?

VIOLA: There's no need to be insulting.

VIOLIN: A slight wound in the arm and you can't play a bit of damned music written by some damned foreigner?

VIOLA: I shall play atrociously.

VIOLIN: All the better. Teach them a lesson. Remember you're a daughter of your country, remember you are a—

VIOLA: Very well.

VIOLIN: Right. Begin, let's get it over.

[CELLO *and* VIOLA *confer.* VIOLIN *stands behind them with his fiddle at the ready.*]

VIOLIN: Go on, then, what are you waiting for? Let the bastards have it.

[CELLO *and* VIOLA *begin to play.*]

VIOLIN: There is a natural and inherent superiority which one country possesses at the expense of all others. That country is, of course, mine. You know it, in your heart of hearts; why don't you admit it?

Not so much a superiority, for this implies a difference of degree. We are not *better* than you at this and that; we are the *best;* everyone else is nowhere and nothing.

Play faster; put some damned beef into it; show them we mean business. One, two, one, two, left, right, left, right! Swell with pride. Make it sound glorious. I don't care if it *was* written by a bloody foreigner; when we play it, it's *ours.* One of the earliest memories I have as a child—

[*A squadron of attackers is heard approaching.*]

VIOLA: They're coming!

VIOLIN: Stand firm! Stand firm!

VIOLA: I'm a civilian. Can't I hoist a white flag?

VIOLIN: Never! A red flag if you like, the colour of blood. There are no civilians, no neutrals, in war there is nothing but war, war. Stand firm. Play louder, faster, faster, pick up the beat, one, two, one, two, left, right, left, right—

[*The attackers peel off and attack.* VIOLA *and* CELLO *play on.* VIOLIN *fires bursts of machine-gun fire from his violin. There is answering fire and the sound of bombs dropping.*]

Play on, play on, play on!!

[VIOLA *gives a scream and falls to the floor.*]

CELLO: They've hit my love!

[*He gets up, takes his cello and sets it up on the floor, crouching beside it. He loads, aims and fires continually. It goes off like an anti-aircraft gun, the recoil jerking him each time. VIOLIN continues firing also.*]

VIOLIN: One of the earliest memories I have as a child . . . is a sense of *wonder* . . . that I had been selected to be one of the fortunate few . . . to be blessed with this particular nationality. Why me, I thought, why me?

[CELLO *is hit, and falls, VIOLIN continues to fire. The attackers disappear. An all-clear sounds. VIOLIN looks round sadly.*]

I think it was then I acquired a sense of mysticism . . .

[*He takes the violin down from his shoulder, looks at it, then wanders about looking for his bow. He finds it, picks it up, and sits down. He puts the violin to his chin in the correct fashion.*]

Though I forget even what nationality it was at the time.

[*He plays a few terrible screeching chords.*]

I've changed it many times since.

[*He attempts more chords.*]

But it's always the same.

[*He cries briefly, plays a chord.*]

Always.

[*He plays a chord or two. A tiny fly is heard around him. He flaps at it with his bow, plays a chord . . .*]

TRIANGLE

a monologue for three
characters

First performance at the Close Theatre, Glasgow, September 1965

ACTOR   Mike Pratt

PROMPTER   Lynn Farleigh

Directed by CLAUDE WHATHAM

CHARACTERS
in order of appearance

ACTOR

PROMPTER

TRIANGLE

[*In the arena is a couch. The* ACTOR *enters. He takes up a position on the couch, reclining on it. Pause.*]

ACTOR: Well, now, Doctor, before we go any further, I think there's something I should tell you. Nothing to do with my case, if that's what you call it, my case, by—on the other hand, I suppose you might conclude that it *is* part of my—case, just another symptom of the same disorder, you might say. I mean, if a man goes to see a priest and the priest says: What is troubling you, my son, and you say: Father, I am in dire spiritual need, having fallen into what you might call the dark pit of spiritual despair from which I can espy no gleam of light—oh, and another thing which I should tell you first of all, I think your church is the equivalent of a load of stinking fish left rotting on a quayside—the Priest is naturally going to assume that this man's attitude to the Church is part of the trouble, if not the cause of it. The fact is, Doctor, you see, I find psychiatry a load of crap. I don't want to offend you, but you obviously want me to be honest. I realise this puts you in a difficult position, since it's necessary I suppose for me to have some sort of faith in you; and you may wonder if I feel like that about your profession why I've put myself into your hands. I wonder too, believe me, but you could put it down to an unconscious *need* to believe if that will help to get the ball rolling. And it does happen constantly to your spiritual equivalent, I'm told, people turning up and saying Christianity is a load of stinking fish, can you help me.

[*He fishes for cigarettes as he reclines, talking meanwhile, finds them and lights one.*]

Well, shall I go into this in a little more detail? It might help us to get acquainted, might it not, and it is after all a small segment of what I would say, if I had to give a flash assessment, is the root of my dilemma, that is to say an inability to hold sacred, or even more, an inability to find meaningful in any way, sacred or profane or what-have-you. Now take your line of country: and for example, let's take this word—association thing; now most patients I imagine wouldn't think much about it, but with me I find myself thinking: well, yes, very clever, but is my unconscious that gullible? Suppose it's cleverer than both of us and when it has to associate with the word—let's say, *beetle*, it comes up naturally with dung, for dung-beetle, realises the possible implications and replaces it before it passes my lips with *butterfly*? Or thinks up butterfly and replaces it with dung, just for the hell of it or to make you happy? Does the unconscious have a sense of humour? Is an unconscious that thinks dung and changes it to butterfly in the same *class* as one that thinks butterfly and changes it to dung? How many bluffs and double-bluffs are going to be played between me and my unconscious and you and *your* unconscious before you get the right answer, if there is a right answer, and anyway what are we sparring about? And so on and so on. I see you're busy writing.

[*He has been fishing with one hand underneath the couch but whatever he wants he doesn't find.*]

The other thing is . . .

[*Pause. He gets up and walks to and fro.*]

He gets up and walks to and fro. To. Fro.

[*He is by the couch. He feels underneath it with his foot.*]

The . . . other . . . thing . . . is . . .

[*The* PROMPTER *sits in the front row of the audience.*]

PROMPTER: These dirty pictures.

[*He doesn't want a prompt. He flaps her away. He coughs, looking at the section of the audience he is facing, turns his head to take in another side of the square.*]

ACTOR [*softly*]: There's a breathless hush in the close tonight, Ten to make and a match to win . . .

[*He goes down on his knees and looks under the couch, which is a very low one. He looks up again, but still on his knees.*]

At this point, I was told, there might be a certain restlessness in the audience. If I may quote: They may evince a certain restlessness.

[*He is on his feet now.*]

ACTOR: Erm . . .

[*He realises that to address the audience he needs four faces: But he turns with indecision (the four sides being equal audience-wise) rather than in panic, and makes what he considers a fair compromise. He coughs again.*]

Ladies and gentlemen, I've thought about this, and I decided to acquaint you at the outset with the idea behind it, there being no rule against it I want to keep this as simple as possible. Erm . . . The erm . . . It's experimental, of course, since that's what you're here for, I believe, and briefly the set-up is like this, and don't blame me for it, I'm only an actor, I erm . . . have been allotted a situation and a character, and some dialogue which I've rehearsed, of course, a playlet, in fact, with no ending, at least it didn't seem like an ending to me. Now this playlet, this fragment lasts about a quarter of an hour, twenty minutes, and I'm supposed to stay here, and of course, you're supposed to stay there for forty. Minutes. Well, you're free to go, which is more than I am. To let you into a secret, it's the first time I've had the length of the performance written into my contract. Forty minutes or no loot. So at least I know the length of my purgatory. Now, the . . .

[*He clears his throat and turns to face, more or less, the remainder of the audience. He looks round quickly.*]

Now the dramatic situation, if you can call it that, is this: I am playing the part—let me get this straight—I am playing an actor who is playing the part of this person, who happens also to be an actor, or *has* to be, erm . . . dealing with this psychiatrist. This one, you can't see him. I am discovered—as they say, discovered on the couch in the waiting, in the psychiatrist's surgery, presumably, erm . . . Under analysis. Or examination. The . . . Let me make one thing clear which I think is rather confusing, which is that the drama written *for* me *included* this element that the, shall I say the drama-actor, I mean the patient, is in fact *in* the play *playing* this part on a stage. Thank you for finding it amusing. In other words, when I, myself, am ad-libbing . . . Well, you'll get the general idea. I hope. Er . . .

[*He grips his nose, apparently thinking. The pause is just long enough to be uncomfortable.*]

PROMPTER: Let me add . . .

[*He removes his hand from his nose. Pause.*]

As a matter of opinion . . .

[*His eyes harden. He stands up and goes to the prompter's side.*]

ACTOR: Look, ducky, when I want a prompt I'll snap. Yes?

[*She nods. He goes back to the couch.*]

Give me a minute or two and I'll get into the swing of it . . . This is S. for sugar, are you receiving me? I've reached the plateau. It's bloody cold up here . . .

[He is not at ease. The joke does not come off.]

I've brought a friend along for company.

[He reaches under the couch and brings out a bottle.]

I arranged for this to be here for three reasons: one of which is that I can take up a little time telling you what the other two are.

[He is now sitting on the couch. He brings out a little glass from his pocket. He puts the glass on the floor and unscrews the bottle top.]

It is not, I trust, generally known that I have achieved in the trade a certain notoriety—or let's say fame, I don't want to brag—as a person not unfond of his bottle. Or anyone else's.

[He puts the bottle down by the glass and stands up, the stopper in his hand.]

My drink is bitter beer followed by whisky chasers. Or whisky followed by bitter beer chasers, depending on whether you think the chicken came first or the egg. Now part of the—

[He drops the stopper. He continues to talk as he picks it up.]

Part of the lonely joy of drinking before a performance is in the skill involved in imbibing enough to bring to the attention of fellow tradesmen and management that you *have* had a few but stopping just short of the point at which they feel justified in remonstrating, or even in putting on the understudy. It keeps them on their toes, you see, and at the same time it makes me feel in some way *superior*. Don't ask why. Now the point of this bit of personal chit-chat is this—let me do it in the form of dialogue. I am here, and the—mind behind this predicament is there. Doctor, get out of the way, you'll confuse the issue.

[He moves to the necessary place for each line.]

Me: What are the rules? Him: Just stay onstage . . . You mean

I can do as I like? . . . Yes . . . Suppose I strip off and utter obscenities? . . . That's all right. Club rules . . . The Lord Chamberlain can't touch you. Only the police. All you have to do is fill up the time. It's up to you. You can lie down on the couch and go to sleep if you like. It's experimental . . . And I'm the guinea pig . . . If you like . . . Well, and aren't you a devil, laddie!

[*He pinches an imaginary cheek.*]

Whereupon he blushes, whether at the barbed compliment or at the touch of my hand on his furry cheek we shall never know. I trust.

[*He crouches at the couch and pours whisky into the glass.*]

And suppose I make it quite clear to the audience which is your dialogue and which is mine? That'll blow the thing sky-high won't it? . . . You can do that if you like . . . Now I may be a bit slow in the uptake, but I didn't get that point till later.

[*He is now standing again, the glass in his hand.*]

So it's in line for me to have a few beforehand? . . . Yes, of course . . . Half-cut? . . . Good idea . . . Pissed? . . . By all means . . .

[*He drains the glass, and looks at it for a moment.*]

So I followed my usual bent, but the joy, strangely, had gone out of it. That is the point of this anecdote, that and passing the time; that apart from the fact that nobody cares or will even *know* if I forget my lines, if they are my lines, and apart from the fact that the only fellow-actor I have to upset is an imaginary head-shrinker who will presumably, in his imaginary way, treat anything I do as just another facet of my case—apart from all this, in accepting this complete freedom on the stage, such as I have never known before, I had lost a component of my freedom *off* it. Not because I was prevented from making the decision to drink, on the contrary I *usually* make no decision, I must have my sequence of drinks, as a matter of habit—but because I was *having* to make a decision, whether to drink or not, and whatever decision I made, whether to drink or not to drink, the result was in some subtle sense planned for in *advance*. *Allowed* for. Do you see? Am I making myself clear?

[*Slight pause. He turns to the audience.*]

I'm giving you all a fair crack of the whip, I hope.

[*He puts the glass down.*]

Forgive me for rambling. As an actor, I'm used to being told what to do. And behaving accordingly, that is either doing it or not doing it. These lines and movements and characterisation tucked away at the back of your head can be very comforting, especially the characterisation. A set of actions all ready made and *OK* and all you have to do is to act them. Erm . . . By which I don't mean there's no choice left for the actor but the choices are, as it were, *contained* inside this framework and are technical ones rather than ethical or—moral ones. Erm . . .

[*Pause.*]

I seem to have lost the thread. As the actress said. Mending the bishop's hassock.
In fact, you see, I'm not quite sure whether I'm trying to play myself or trying *not* to play myself . . .

[*He pours a drink and drinks it.*]

Anyway you don't want a lecture, and I don't want to use all my ideas up in one fell swoop, or is it sweep, and then have to use up the dialogue and then be faced with a yawning chasm which is myself, naked on the stage, so to speak.

[*He sits down. Pause.*]

Anyway, not to be outdone . . . Overwhelmed, you might say, by the great—void of freedom into which I was to be allowed to step, leap, fall headlong . . .

[*He chuckles.*]

I thought of a ruse . . . Dashing in its conception and beautiful in its simplicity . . . Something to put me again on top. Where I like to be . . . Namely, to secrete a bottle, which does not contain cold tea, under an item of stage furniture. Or have secreted, by the good offices of a stage-hand. That I have only chaser and no chased, the hunter you might say without the quarry, or the chased without the unchased can't be helped, since my ingenuity didn't run to getting a barrel under there while the manipulation of two discrete—D-I-S-C-R-E-T-E bottles might compound the confusion and lead to breakages.

[*He checks his watch.*]

One answer would have been a trained St. Bernard.

[*From now on he drinks as he thinks fit.*]

No, wait! Let me use my freedom . . . Let there be an *imaginary* firkin of bitter, which as you all know contains nine imaginary gallons, just there. Standing on an imaginary stool, and owned by the psychiatrist. So he can drink his imaginary beer while I drink my imaginary cold tea, and then *I* imaginarily chase it with his imaginary beer while he imaginarily chases his with my scotch. That puts me one up on him for a start, since I'd rather be drinking imaginary cold tea which is whisky than drinking in my imagination real whisky which is nothing. And that's sucked that one dry.

[*Slight pause.*]

Let me assure you—

[*He decides to give the other side of the audience a turn.*]

Let me assure you that . . . however . . . I am not so naive as—
not to realise, double negative, that my victory, I don't mean
over my psychiatric friend there but over this other fellow,
my manipulator who pretends to be my liberator . . . is a
hollow one, imaginary . . . I'm sorry—rather than real. For
my . . . Ah, now this is clever. My victory consists in the fact
that I have . . . What's the word . . . ?

[*He snaps his finger.*]

PROMPTER: Transgressed?

[*He glares at her. She bites her lip.*]

ACTOR: As you like. Transgressed. But how—you may ask . .
And you may not . . .

[*Pause.*]

As a matter of fact these were not his only words on the subject. 'They may evince a certain restlessness', he said, in his high
voice, 'And on the other hand they may sit there like a lot of
turds.' Yes, that was the *mot* with which he chose to describe
his audience. My audience. His word, not mine.

[*He thinks for a moment. He stands up to continue, and walks about.*]

All right, to continue: How, you may ask, can one transgress
when there are no rules? Answer:

[*He puts his hands over his eyes and stands still to get it right.*]

Answer: by assuming that there are no rules *because* it is
assumed that I won't break them. That's not very clear. Again.
By assuming that there *are* rules, but that I was not considered
—big enough, daring enough; decadent enough to find out
what they are and therefore break them. Or break them and
therefore find out what they are. That's better. But still confusing. You're confused. So am I. Let us persevere. By assum-

ing that—I am considered small. Minor. A small person, an actor, whose horizons are limited—by his nature. Ah. Wait. We're on to something big here, Carruthers.

[*Slight pause.*]

As the lion-tamer said to the . . . contortionist. In the tent of the Fat Lady.

[*Slight pause.*]

Yes. The point is this: I am *allowed* to do anything because I am not *expected* to do anything. As you would allow, let's say, a babe in blue swaddling clothes to romp at will with his sibling in pink swaddling clothes tucked up in the same twin pram. No holds barred. If they suddenly ripped the swaddles off and gave themselves to incest, what a smack in the eye for someone then. I am given full license . . . allow me to labour the point—because my manipulator . . . My inky-fingered God . . . can think of nothing I could do which might shock him. I won't strip naked and utter obscenities, he knows that; so he can allow it. Bountiful, bountiful. Such is my freedom. And this is why I said my victory is a hollow one because . . . because the transgression is in my imagination only, knowing as I do that had I *said* I meant to secrete a bottle of scotch under the couch he would have answered: Yes, of course; good idea; by all means . . .

[*He wanders back to the couch.*]

The power is therefore *his*, not mine. D'you see? He would say, with a smirk, he has released me; as the shepherd releases his sheepdog, and what does the sheepdog do then, poor thing, in its sublime freedom? Run to and fro to the whistle, salivate to the ball, and crap discreetly when his work is done. R-double E-T. My master has opened the cage, and I hurtle forth to the end!—of my little chain!

And if that is my freedom and that is his power—where is the glory?... Rhetorical question...

[*Slight pause.*]

All this over a bottle.

[*He changes his position and broods. He suddenly turns to encompass the whole of the audience with his eyes. He takes out a cigarette, the last in the packet. He throws the empty packet down and lights the cigarette. He is lost in thought for a moment.*]

Dramatic highlight number one. What a blade I am, what a devil...

[*Pause. He stands on the couch.*]

There's a breathless hush in the close tonight!
Ten to make and the match to win—
A bumping pitch and a blinding light,
An hour to play and the last man in.
And it's not for the sake of a ribboned coat,
Or the selfish hope of a season's fame,
But his Captain's hand on his shoulder smote—
'Play up: play up! and play the game!'
Yes, Herr Doktor? Don't you agree? Mein mitteleuropaischer Freund? His name is, er—Schittel, Dr Schittel, und he schpeak mit ein *accent*, zo ... I have decided. If I am to be manipulated I shall manipulate in my turn, be it only a figment. Stand up, Herr Doktor! Sit down, Herr Doktor! Stand up. Sit down, stand down,—ah!

[*He wags a gleeful finger at the* DOCTOR.]

Drop your trousers, Herr Doktor!

[*To the audience.*]

Have no fear. All I want is power. With his trousers up he's the mysterious Doctor; with them down round his ankles, he's a figure of fun. So much for the dignity of Man.

[*He gets off the couch.*]

I know what you're thinking. You're thinking that even this wraith which I claim for my own was conceived by my— good shepherd and shaped in his substance or lack of it by countless bad films, a TV serial or two and half a dozen horror comics. But you're wrong. That's only the raw material. What matters is what you do with it, as the actress said. And who knows—who knows but that out of my febrile and pullulating brain, or do I mean suppurating? I may fashion myself a creature to call my own, a creature so dreadful and so vivid in the certainty of his own existence which *I* have planted in his non-existent head—and how do I know *I* exist except that someone has done the same for me . . . that he o'erleaps the puny bounds of reason, I have played Shakespeare, breaks down the bastion of probability and to the hosts of turdish eyes set in their turdish faces cries aloud: God for Harry, England and St George, I am Schittel! Who wants to make something of it? Then leaping amongst the audience with his hook, his claw and his surgeon's knife, slashes, rapes, castrates and scares the living *shit* out of the lot of you!

[*He sits down.*]

And me, and me.

[*He closes his eyes. Long pause. He then snaps his fingers once. No response. He opens his eyes and looks, more in sorrow than in anger, at the* PROMPTER. *She is looking down, though not, of course, following the script. She looks up eventually and sees his eyes on her. He very deliberately raises his hands and snaps his fingers.*]

PROMPTER: The other thing is . . .

[*He continues to look at her with sad eyes.*]

These dirty pictures . . .

[*He continues to look at her with sad eyes.*]

These blots . . .

[*He continues to look at her with sad eyes. Then he swivels round, lies back on the couch and closes his eyes. He snaps his fingers.*]

Now you say . . .

[*He snaps his fingers.*]

They're random patterns . . .

[*He snaps his fingers.*]

But anyone can see . . .

[*He snaps his finger. No response. He snaps again. No response. Pause. He suddenly snaps his fingers.*]

The other thing is . . .

[*He raises his arm in despair and lets it fall. Pause. He may begin to sing. Then, still at first with his eyes closed. . .*]

ACTOR: The other thing is those dirty pictures, Herr Doktor. These blots. Now you say they're random patterns, but anyone can see they're really dirty pictures. If you chain a chimpanzee to a piano for long enough he'll play Beethoven, though I hate to think of the state the place would be in by then, and if you train enough blots to make random patterns some of these blots, Herr Doktor, will be flowers and pretty flying things whilst another proportion will be fiendishly obscene graffiti from the steaming walls of hell's own urinals, like that—two-headed monster copulating with a reindeer which you were kind enough to show to me. No, Schittel, you're the one I condemn, not for your filthy-mindedness but for your hypocrisy. *You* know that's a two-headed monster copulating with a reindeer, don't you? Don't you? My God, I bet you *drew* it. Or *posed* for it. You'd only need to remove one of your heads. And I'll bet you show them to lady psychiatrists in dark corners too, you pervert. I come here to be healed and what do I find, a pit of vice. Will you put that bloody notebook down!

[*He has said all this without raising his head to look at the* DOCTOR. *There is a pause.*]

If I were a writer, instead of *merely* an actor, the one thing I would not write about would be guess what—a psychiatrist.

[*He sits up. From now on he is on his own. He can, of course, have a fresh packet of cigarettes in his pocket if he wishes.*]

Not because these characters are old *hat*, but because even when they were *new* hat they were, what's the word, ducky, quite right, phoney, and also that other word, despicable, that's the one. Isn't that right, Schittel? You know it's true deep down inside, don't you, that you're as phoney as the day is long and as despicable as the night—your special province, Schittel, filled with wet Freudian dreams of other people's wives or even the wives themselves—as the night is short? Ladies and gentlemen, I once knew—no, I didn't know, I met briefly, a head-shrinker, I'm not going to tell you what his name was, but one fact about him, among many, was that he was a Kraut, I beg your pardon, of Germanic stock, which made him even more of a cliché than usual. And I've just realised . . .

[*He stops and laughs.*]

Oh dear, oh dear, I must be *very* slow in the uptake. I have just realised what is expected of me.

[*He laughs again.*]

You know already, of course. You've twigged. Put an actor on the stage, put an audience all round, block the exits, don't give him lines and characterisation and plot or any of that junk, but just a great big public vacuum to fill, oh, and a bottle of cold tea which turns out to be whisky, and I wonder what he'll do this actor playing an actor, all alone in a cage without bars, if there were bars you couldn't see so well, could you, and no one but an imaginary fucking mind-doctor for company—ah, that shocked you! That did it. I felt a little tremor there, like at the zoo when a monkey does something particularly disgusting. Whatever will he do next? Why don't you throw me a nut, madam? Maybe I'll stuff it up my arse. The word, however, the epithet, was well chosen, believe me. No, don't believe me, it wasn't chosen at all, but it was apt all the same, wasn't it, Schittel? Yes, I wondered why you were all so quiet. So they must have sat round the guillotine, knitting needles hushed for a moment as the climax came. What a marvellous part that must have been to play, the aristocrat in the tumbril. ' 'Tis a far, far better thing I do—' Oh, great, a great performance. Even the lunatics in the asylums, they must have acted it up. That's the one great quality of madness, it's such a marvellous part to play to the right audience. But I'm sorry—ladies and gentlemen—but I beg to be excused. I am too good an actor ever to play such a dull character as myself. I am not familiar with the part.

[*He chuckles. And looks at his watch.*]

So you may as well go home, file out quietly, the show is over. To those who remain I shall talk about mundane matters, like those school compositions we used to do in the far-off days when life was simple. A Day in the Country. What I Did In My Last Hols, oh, no, you won't have that one. A Film I Saw

Recently. And if you're good I'll tell you an undramatic anecdote. But more interesting than the one in the script.

So you may go home, my dear, I shall not require your services any longer. Oh, what a marvellous job it must be, prompting, Not only a member of an audience, but a *knowing* member of an audience. Sitting there quietly with my part at her finger-tips, I'm not trying to be dirty, knowing every word and movement I should make and all ready to correct me if I go wrong. But you're a bit lost today, aren't you, dear? It's not in the book. Never mind, you can sit like the rest of them, my observers, my judges, sit with cold detached eyes and wait for me to what? Make a fool of myself? Unmask myself? Dance naked before you? So that you can *really* judge me, not for my performance but for what I am? I tell you what, come up here, come out of your safe little burrow, your little observation post, and we'll dance naked together. Shall we? No? You've been at my cold tea again, Schittel.

Art is not life, ladies and gentlemen. Believe me. I say I am too good an actor to play myself, and you know what I mean. You're actors too. Better ones than I am, let's face it, I'm a bit on the bravura side, but you, you give superlative perfor-mances, you really do, beautiful. With not a chink in the armour. So you know what I mean. The good actor never has to play himself and we're all good actors. Because, ladies and gentlemen, my friends . . . If you scratch an actor, what will you find? Another actor underneath, that's right. I'm a professional, that's all the difference. And if you scratch for long enough, what will you find? A little person. Like that. A little wee person, too wee and certainly too undramatic to even feel sorry for. Who works on wires, like that. A little person who tries not to notice the wires and tries to think of himself some-times as having a certain *importance* and a certain uniqueness and a certain *nobility* . . . Poor thing . . . And tries to judge: because to judge, of course, is the only possible way he has, this poor little fellow, to puff himself up a little. That and not noticing the wires . . . And then he catches sight of himself again . . .

[*Pause. He looks at his watch, and perhaps shakes it.*]

I've just remembered I brought a prop with me.

[*He fishes in his pocket while he speaks and brings out a stage dagger.*]

I meant to play a naughty trick on you. You see?

[*He shows how the blade retracts.*]

I meant to work it up to a big bravura crescendo, the big actor bit, you know? And then stab myself with my stage dagger. Only I forgot . . .

[*Pause.*]

All right. Undramatic anecdote: this anecdote concerns this head-shrinker I think I mentioned, this Kraut called Schittel, no, not Schittel. Did I tell you he had no back to his head? I mean he had a —flat, here—

[*He slaps the back of his head.*]

—as if when he was a child he spent much of his time leaning with his soft childish head against a brick wall. Maybe he did for all I know, as I told you I met him only once, this Kraut. Now . . . This anecdote really concerns a friend of mine. Well, an acquaintance. It concerns this acquaintance and his wife, and the psychiatrist. It's quite short. What happens, you see, the wife went to the psychiatrist. Ah, now the *reason* she went to the psychiatrist was on account of the husband, this acquaintance of mine, who was at that time having an affair with a third party—fourth party, who doesn't enter into this anecdote except as already mentioned. Don't misunderstand, this man got on very well with his wife, he told me, or he had through all the other affairs. But on this occassion, for reasons he could not or would not divulge to me, he wanted to tell his wife about it, and it preyed on his mind, wanting to tell his wife and not being able to. And since his wife knew in any case, their relationship became strained, and the wife finally went to see the psychiatrist. She told the psychiatrist all about her marriage, you know, all the details, and all about all his other affairs which in fact she'd known all along, and the psychiatrist said, well what do you want? And she said, I want to behave in a sensible way and not to have to bother when my husband has these affairs since he's a free man and this is the twentieth century and I can see they're necessary to him and why not? So he got her down on his couch and she told him a lot of other details all about her marriage and her husband and all. And then he seduced her; or she seduced him, or it was what they call a spontaneous conflagration, you get the general picture, the husband was a bit vague on this point. Maybe the psychiatrist showed her some of his dirty blots, I don't know. Anyway, after six months of this treatment, lo and behold she was, cured. So she said to her husband, it's all right now, you can do as you like, and told him what had been happening on the couch. Well, actually the bed, the couch would have been unethical and was only a single couch in any case.

[*He sits on the couch.*]

End of undramatic anecdote. I'd like to be able to inform you that it broke this chap's heart; but that would be dramatic. So it didn't really do anything to him. He carried on with his affair, which he didn't now have to tell his wife about because she knew; and she carried on with hers. Of course, being an acquaintance of mine, he was an actor, and being an actor,

when he'd finished telling me this anecdote, I don't know
what was going on with his little fellow inside, but the outside
actor, the one on top . . . cried . . .

[*He puts his hands over his face.*]

. . . like this . . . like this . . .

[*Blackout.*]

ALAS, POOR FRED

First performance at the Theatre-in-the-Round, Scarborough, Summer 1959

PRINGLE	William Elmhurst
MRS PRINGLE	Dona Martyn

Directed by RODNEY WOOD

CHARACTERS
in order of appearance

PRINGLE

MRS PRINGLE

ALAS, POOR FRED

[*A drawing room.* PRINGLE *sits in his easy chair, head back, eyes closed. In the other easy chair* MRS PRINGLE *knits. All is peace.*]

PRINGLE: I can't get over poor Fred.
MRS: It's best not thought about.
PRINGLE: That's true . . .

[*There is a pause.*]

It seems like only yesterday.
MRS: Time plays funny tricks
PRINGLE: As the poet says: When . . . [*he lifts his hands, but drops them again. There is a pause.*]
MRS: Well, he's out of it now. That's the way I look at it.
PRINGLE: One has to be philosophical. Otherwise . . .
MRS: It must be funny to be cut in half . . . Without any warning. Funny . . .
PRINGLE: I don't think so. *Odd*, I'd say. Decidedly *odd*. I wouldn't say quite *funny*.
MRS: I mean *odd*.
PRINGLE: Oh, yes, I see. I thought you meant funny. You meant *odd*.
MRS: I mean *odd*, yes.
PRINGLE: Well, yes, most odd, I'd say. Most decidedly odd . . . And *almost* funny, you know, when you think about it. Not quite, but *almost*.
MRS [*considering*]: No . . . No, I don't think so. Not funny. *Odd*, I think, very odd, but I don't think quite funny.
PRINGLE: You don't think so?
MRS: No, I don't think so. After all . . .
PRINGLE: Yes, you're probably right.
MRS: One has to respect his memory.
PRINGLE: Naturally, of course. One has to be Christian.

MRS: R.I.P. That's what I say.

PRINGLE: Very true ... [*he yawns*] Did I ever have that cocoa?

MRS: What cocoa?

PRINGLE: Wasn't there something about a cup of cocoa? I seem to remember ...

MRS: What time is it?

PRINGLE [*looking at his watch*]: Of course, since I don't remember whether I had it or not I suppose it doesn't matter ... It's a little unsettling, though, not knowing.

MRS: Shall I make you another cup?

PRINGLE: Another?

MRS: In case you didn't have the first one.

PRINGLE: No, let it lie. It'll die out ... Fred, of course, was never blessed with a sense of humour.

MRS: He was a good man.

PRINGLE: Oh yes. No question of that.

MRS: A Christian.

PRINGLE: Right through, absolutely.

MRS: He went to church regularly. Every Christmas Day.

PRINGLE: He was a good man all right. I grant you that ... But he hadn't what you could call a sense of humour.

MRS: His collar was as stiff as a poker. And he never unrolled his umbrella, even when it rained ... He was an Englishman. There's no gainsaying it.

PRINGLE: That's true, of course.

MRS: You can say what you like about him, but you can't deny this: he always kept his moustache straight. It says a lot for a man.

PRINGLE: He what?

MRS: Whatever else he was, he kept his moustache straight.

PRINGLE: Moustache? What moustache?

MRS: *His* moustache.

PRINGLE: He had no moustache.

MRS: What?

PRINGLE: He had *no* moustache.

MRS: I'm talking about Fred.

PRINGLE: Yes, Fred. That's right. He had no moustache. He was cleanshaven.

MRS: Fred had no moustache?

PRINGLE: He had *whiskers* growing out of his *nose*.

MRS: Fred?

PRINGLE: Not whiskers. Hairs. Quite long hairs. Almost whiskers. But not what you could call a moustache. He had no moustache.

MRS: Of course he had a moustache. A long straight one.

PRINGLE: No, dear.

MRS: What are you trying to do to me?

PRINGLE: I'm only saying, dear, he had no moustache . . .

MRS: In other words you're saying he was cleanshaven.

PRINGLE: Well, if you like to put it that way . . .

MRS: So it's come to this . . .

PRINGLE: *Whiskers*, dear. Out of his nose.

MRS: Whiskers, he had no whiskers.

PRINGLE: Well, hairs.

MRS: No hairs.

PRINGLE: Do you mean to tell me he had no hairs growing out of his nose?

MRS: None.

PRINGLE: *Fred*.

MRS: Fred . . .

PRINGLE: I don't know what to say . . .

MRS: I never heard of such a thing . . .

[*There is a pause.*]

It was this long.

PRINGLE: His moustache?

MRS: Certainly.

PRINGLE: What colour?

MRS: Oh, a sort of . . . brown.

PRINGLE: No.

MRS: I don't know how you can sit there and look me in the eye and say he had no moustache.

PRINGLE: It's not a question of looking you in the eye.

MRS: I think it is. That's what I think. I think that's just what it is. I'm sorry.

PRINGLE: I'm sorry too. We've obviously reached a point of disagreement. That's what it seems to me.

MRS: It's not a question of . . .

PRINGLE: I'm sorry, but that's the way I see it. I can't see it in any other light. We hold different views on the matter. You think one thing and I think another, that's the way it appears to me. We hold divergent opinions on the subject. That's putting it in a nutshell.

MRS: That's all very well.

PRINGLE: I may be wrong, but as far as I can make out this is the position; you say one thing and I say something else. That's all there is to it.

MRS: I only say—

PRINGLE: Exactly. Very well. You have it your way and I'll have it mine. That's all there is to be said. It's no use arguing. If you think Fred had a moustache you must do so. We could go on arguing about it until we were black in the face and still be no nearer a solution. The only thing to be done is forget the whole subject. [*He rests his head back and closes his eyes.*]

MRS: Very well. If that's the way you feel about it we'll not mention it again. It's obviously a bone of contention. It always has been . . .

[*She knits. Silence.* PRINGLE *suddenly sits up.*]

PRINGLE: If Fred had a moustache, what about the photograph which was taken of him on the promenade at Sandwich in 1925? Hey? Answer me that.

[*She continues to knit without looking up.*]

Ah, there. You see. So. [*He retires triumphantly to his original position.*]

MRS: He never went to Sandwich.

PRINGLE [*sitting up*]: What!

MRS: You are mistaken. He never went to Sandwich.

PRINGLE: But the photograph. Are you sitting there in that chair telling me that he never went to Sandwich?

MRS: Rye.

PRINGLE: Not Rye, Sandwich!

MRS: No.

PRINGLE: Yes, yes!

MRS: Winchelsea. Rye. Not Sandwich. He disliked Sandwich.

PRINGLE: How could he dislike Sandwich if he never went there? Answer me that!

MRS: He disliked the name. He'd never even *eat* a Sandwich, let alone *go* to Sandwich.

PRINGLE: You are telling me he never ate sandwiches?

MRS: Never.

PRINGLE: I don't know what to say . . . I'm dumbfounded . . . *Fred*.

MRS: Fred.

PRINGLE: My dear Ethel, ham sandwiches were his favourite food.

MRS: Ham. Not sandwiches.

PRINGLE: In 1925, on the promenade, at Sandwich, in the company of yourself and myself, Fred had his photograph taken while *eating a ham sandwich*!

MRS: No, Ernest. Not Sandwich. Not Fred. Not 1925. Not a sandwich.

PRINGLE: I don't know what to say.

MRS: *Deal*, perhaps. 1924 perhaps. Eating a roll. With Tom. Not Fred.

PRINGLE: I know nobody called Tom.

MRS: In that case, I can't help you. It's your memory, Ernest. You must sort it out for yourself.

PRINGLE: You deny that Fred was photographed on the promenade at Sandwich in 1925 eating a Sandwich?

MRS: I think there's nothing more to be said.

PRINGLE: Oh. So. Really. We'll see about that. We shall ascertain whether that is the case. [*He gets up and goes to the door.*]

MRS: What are you going to do?

PRINGLE: I am going to fetch the photograph. [*He goes out.*]

MRS: Why must it always come to this? . . . Every night is the same. Sometimes I get a feeling of impending doom even before the sun goes down. But the doom never arrives. How is that, I wonder? [*She knits, then stops.*] One thing I hope for. That is, that one evening Ernest will go out of the room for some reason, as he does occasionally during the evening, and that while I am sitting here alone in the quiet room that chair . . . will move. Just a little. I don't want it to move much. Just a foot, or six inches, without any noise or fuss. What a thing that would be . . . Ernest would come back and I should say, Ernest, something happened while you were away. And he'd say nonsense, nothing happened. And I'd say yes, Ernest, *this* time something did happen while you were away. And he'd say, what could happen while I was away? And I'd say, I'll give you three guesses, Ernest, what happened, and if you guess right you can wish for anything you want and I'll make it come true, and he'd say, did the clock stop? No, that's one. Did the pictures slip out of square? No, Ernest darling, the picture didn't slip out of square, and that's two. Now here's your last one and you must guess carefully because if you guess wrong I shall have to tell you and you won't believe me and you won't get your wish either, and he'd say, well now, I guess that that chair . . . moved. Yes, darling, I'd say, yes, darling, Ernest darling, that's just exactly what happened. That's just exactly what happened, darling Ernest darling, you have your wish. Who cares about old chairs. Take me in your arms, darling Ernest darling, and do with me what thou wilt . . . But it never does, needless to say.

[*She knits.* PRINGLE *comes in with a huge box, which he puts on the table.*]

PRINGLE: Now . . . [*He opens the box.*] We shall see. [*He takes out a photograph album, which he puts on the table, then another then another, then another, then a photograph. This he studies for a moment, close up, then takes it to the window to study it better.*] Has anyone seen my glasses?

MRS: You've got them on, dear.

PRINGLE: What, On, yes. Yes, yes, of course I have. [*He looks at the photograph again.*] Yes, yes, that's better . . . You know, Ethel, in her day your grandmother's sister was really a very fine figure of a woman . . . And only married once. Remarkable. [*He puts the photograph down.*] Yet your grandfather's brother was anything but prepossessing, and he was married three times, to one woman and another. It's strange the way things turn out . . . Well, well, we live in the world that we live in, so we might as well make the best of it. That's what I say.

MRS: My father used to say that.

PRINGLE: And my mother. Ernest, she used to say, we live in the world that we live in, so we might as well make the best of it. That's what I say. I take after my mother, you know, more than I take after my father. Ernest, my father used to say to me after Sunday dinner which in those days of course was a proper *Sunday* dinner you know, I mean a real Sunday *dinner*, not the sort of Sunday dinner one gets nowadays but a real *Sunday dinner*, with carrots and greens and beans in butter, we *always* had beans, my father was particularly partial to beans, I remember one Saturday my mother said to me, Ernest, we've got no beans for tomorrow, for the love of God run round the corner to Mrs Bird, that was Mrs Bird who lived round the corner in Sheep's Lane that *was*, before they turned it into a block of flats, of course there's nothing left of it now.

[*There is a pause.* MRS PRINGLE *knits away.*]

. . . and ask if she's got some beans or there'll be the devil to pay tomorrow. [*There is another pause.*] . . . and beef, of course, always beef, and boiled potatoes and baked potatoes, that is *roast* potatoes only we always called them baked potatoes. Baked potatoes we called potatoes baked in their jackets . . . And batter pudding, that is to say Yorkshire pudding, only we always called it batter pudding . . . Batter pudding we called just batter . . . And gravy . . . [*There is another pause.*] Poor old dad . . . It wasn't much of a life . . . But he ate.

[*There is a pause.*]

MRS: Do you want to listen to the nine o'clock news?

PRINGLE: No, no, no . . . Ah! [*He has found another photograph.*] Now. See. Here. [*He brings the photogarph over to* MRS PRINGLE.] Now. Let us be quite sure on the matter. *You* say Fred did *not* have his photograph taken on the promenade at Sandwich in 1925 in the company of yourself and myself, cleanshaven and eating a ham sandwich, correct?

MRS: Oh, Ernest, must we go through all this again?

PRINGLE: Whereas *I* say that in 1925 at Sandwich eating a ham sandwich in the company of yourself and myself, Fred *was* photographed on the promenade, cleanshaven. Would you or would you not say that that is a fair and accurate statement of the argument?

MRS: Oh, Ernest . . .

PRINGLE: Come come come, yes or no. Yes or no. Come come. Come come come. Come come. Yes or no.

MRS: If only I could go mad, just for once. Not just half mad, not just a little dazed, but really, really and truly mad . . . If only I could leap over the battlements of my sanity and . . . and . . .

What would I do? Yes . . . I should unravel my knitting. I should unravel my knitting, every stitch. Delicious madness. Then drawing myself up to my full height, my mad eyes blazing with suppressed desire, I should say: Ernest I should say, you have deceived me, in a voice quivering with emotion. You have played me false. False. False. There you stand, talking about photographs of my grandmother's sister, there you stand; but I have my memories. Thirty years ago you swore to love me and no other; to love me and cherish me and abide with me. And so you did, you kept your promise. For thirty years you have been faithful to me, as I to you. You have ministered to my needs, you have fed and clothed me and unclothed me. And I can stand it no longer. Saying which I should take my knitting needle and plunge it into his heart, and then into my own. So die all faithful couples. Slowly our life's blood would mingle on the carpet . . .

PRINGLE: Mrs Pringle, you are not paying attention.

MRS: Yes, dear.

PRINGLE: Now, what was I talking about? [*They look at each other. There is a pause.*] This is really too bad!. [*He begins to pace up and down.*] You see what a pass we've been brought to now.

MRS: If only the world could come to an end quite suddenly.

PRINGLE: I have it. I remember. All is well.

MRS: Oh God! . . .

PRINGLE: Look at his photograph. [*He hands it to her.*] See. Yourself. Myself. Fred. Eating a ham sandwich. Cleanshaven. Now look at the back. What does it say?

MRS: Have pity on me . . . !

PRINGLE: The promenade, Sandwich, 1925 . . . The Promenade, Sandwich, 1925. [*He turns the photograph over again.*] Yourself. Myself. Fred. No moustache. Ham sandwich. The promenade, Sandwich, 1925. Fred, yourself, myself. Cleanshaven. Ham sandwich, 1925. The promenade, Sandwich. Fred. No moustache. Ham sandwich.

[*They look at each other for a moment, then* PRINGLE *slams victoriously to his chair, sits down, sits back, and closes his eyes.* MRS PRINGLE *resumes her knitting. There is a pause.*]

MRS: If it were.   [B . O .]

[*A pause.*]

PRINGLE: What?
MRS: Fred.
PRINGLE: If Fred were what?
MRS: If it were Fred.
PRINGLE: If what were Fred.
MRS: If it were *Fred*.

[*There is a pause. Then* PRINGLE *sits up, looks at* MRS PRINGLE *for a moment, gets up, takes the photograph, looks at it.*]

PRINGLE: If this is not Fred, then who the devil is it? Answer me that.
MRS: Bill.
PRINGLE: Bill who?
MRS: Bill Quink.
PRINGLE: But Bill Quink had a moustache. This man is cleanshaven.
MRS: No, dear. Bill Quink was cleanshaven. *Sam* Quink had a moustache.
PRINGLE: I didn't know there *was* a Sam Quink. I thought it was *Bill* Quink. And *Bill* Quink I thought was *Bill* Quink. Which was correct of course. But confusing. I always wanted to get to the bottom of that moustache. Well well well! So he had a moustache all the time.
MRS: No, dear. Bill Quink was cleanshaven.
PRINGLE: Yes, I know, dear. But he had a moustache. But he was *Sam* Quink. You see . . .
MRS: Shall I make you a cup of coffee?

PRINGLE: This is most interesting. Let me see that photograph again . . . [*He examines the photograph.*] Yes, yes, Ethel. I think you're right. I really think you're right. This is Bill Quink. Of course it's hard to recognise him without his moustache.

MRS: No, dear. Bill Quink was cleanshaven. . .

PRINGLE: That's what I'm saying, dear . . .

MRS: Oh, yes . . .

PRINGLE: Well, well, well, it just goes to show.

MRS: As my mother used to say.

PRINGLE: Your mother? Nonsense, dear!

MRS: But, Ernest . . .

PRINGLE: Your mother never said that. My father said it.

MRS: But no, Ernest, it was my mother said that . . .

PRINGLE: Ethel, am I to be master in my own house or not?

[*There is a pause.* MRS PRINGLE *knits.*]

I've never heard of such a thing. There you sit contradicting me at every turn. One minute you promise to love, honour and obey me, and the next minute, what happens? You contradict my every word. Well, as my father used to say, it just goes to show. It was the same for him, just the same. If he even so much as wanted a wash, be it morning, afternoon or evening, especially in the evening, I've known it happen in the evening many a time. Many and many a time. It just goes to show, that's all I can say . . .

[*There is a pause.*]

PRINGLE: ⎱ Yes, if he even so much as wanted a wash—
MRS: ⎰ Perhaps a cheese sandwich would be a—

[*They both stop.* PRINGLE *blows his nose noisily.*]

PRINGLE: ⎱ Yes, if he even so much as wanted a *wash*—
MRS: ⎰ Perhaps a cheese sandwich would be a—

[*They both stop.* PRINGLE *quivers with indignation.* MRS PRINGLE *puts her hand to her mouth.* PRINGLE *flings himself into his chair.* MRS PRINGLE *knits nervously. There is a long pause.* MRS PRINGLE *opens her mouth but shuts it again. There is a pause.*]

[*They both stop.* PRINGLE *is speechless. He draws in his br at , looks round the room violently, walks across the room and noisily lifts a chair and replaces it. He then goes to the windows and draws the curtains so violently that they sail the off end of their rod and collapse at his feet.*]

PRINGLE: I've had enough of it, do you hear . . . Your cousin's husband is a mannerless pig, and your mother's aunt has no taste in hats!

[*He marches to the door and opens it.*]

MRS: Go on, throw that in my face again.

PRINGLE: I am going to take Fido for a walk! Round the block!

[*With which he slams the door.*]

MRS: Fido died three years ago. In any case his name was Susie. She was a bitch . . . [*She knits.*] The front door's a long time slamming. He can't find the lead . . .

[*The front door slams.*]

He's found it . . .

[*She knits. There is a loud knock at the front door.*]

He's forgotten his key . . . Well, he shall wait. He isn't the only one . . . I shall count up to ten, and *then* I shall go. One—two—three—four—five—six—seven—eight—nine— [*She listens.*] That's his key in the lock . . . Yes, he's opened the door. So he found he had his key after all. But then why is he opening the door? . . . Could he not have realised he's found his key, and still be coming in to find it? . . . After all, his spectacles were on his nose. The difference is the same . . . But then why is he waiting in the hall? . . . Perhaps he's now realised he's found the key he came back for . . . Then why doesn't he go out again? Has he lost the lead while he was looking for the key? But that would be *outside*, and he's *inside* . . . Perhaps he's gone Perhaps he went out quietly and I didn't . . . Perhaps he didn't come back at all! That's it. Perhaps the whole thing, the whole thing is in my *imagination*. Am I going mad at last? [*She listens.*] No sound . . . Goodness gracious me, perhaps I only *imagine* that I imagined that it happened . . . I'll knit a little and see . . . [*She knits, then stops.*] I can still knit . . . Unless I'm imagining that I'm knitting . . . [*She knits, then stops.*] But if I can *imagine* myself knitting, I can *knit*, I should think . . . No, he really knocked. He's still there . . . Perhaps he's waiting to murder me. Strangle me with the lead . . . No, he wouldn't do that . . . Goodness gracious me above us, of course! I see. Yes, yes, this is the way it is; he went out. He remembered he's forgotten his key. He knocked. While he was waiting he remembered he hadn't forgotten the key. It was in his pocket all the time. So he opened the door to tell me not to bother to let him in because he's found the key after all. Yes, yes, it all fits into place. *But* . . . when he got inside a thought struck him; why hadn't I opened the door when he knocked? Perhaps I was ill, perhaps I'd had a seizure. Perhaps I was sitting slumped over my knitting, the life's blood draining away from my pallid cheeks. Ethel, what have I done to you? Has it come to this? Am I never to see those . . . ? On the other hand, the thought struck him: Perhaps she simply didn't *want* to open the door. Perhaps she's just sitting there, with nothing the matter with her at all, saying to herself, why *should* I open the door; let him wait. Ah. So. That's the way, it is. Very well. Two can play at that game. If she think's I'm . . . But of course she *might* be . . . impossible. She never has seizures. She even has her own teeth. Seizures, ha, ha, what an idea? So she thinks I'm going to think she's had a seizure, does she? Ha ha . . . But on the other hand, good gracious, what am I to do now? If I go into the room after standing here for so long it'll look funny. What could I say I've been doing? Wondering whether she's had a seizure or not? So, she'd say, you stand out there in the hall, waiting for me to die. So that's the way of it. But then, if I go out that'll seem funny too. To knock on the door, open it, stand in the hall, and then go out again . . . No, that would seem very funny . . . Whatever I do now it'll seem funny. I'm in a predicament, that's what I'm in, a dilemma. I've placed myself in such a position that my next move is *bound* to be ridiculous. That's a terrible position for a man to be placed in. Of course, *she* may perhaps be thinking that I've had a seizure . . . No, no, The best thing to do is to put a brave face on it. If I go out now and slam the door and walk about for a while, by the time I come back we can both pretend we've forgotten about it. Yes, yes, that's the only way. I'll count up to ten, then I'll go out quickly and slam the door . . . One—two—three—four—five—six—seven—eight—nine—

[*A knock on the door.*]

My goodness gracious me, someone at the door! He's trapped! . . . No, wait. Somebody's opening the door. With a key. From *outside*! . . .

[*The door slams.*]

It's a plot! A plot to kill me!

[*The room door opens and* PRINGLE *comes in.*]

Did you have a nice walk, dear? [*Knitting*]
PRINGLE: I didn't go.
MRS: [*knitting*]: Oh!
PRINGLE: A very funny thing happened. First I couldn't find the lead; then as soon as I had closed the front door I remembered

I'd forgotten the door key. So I knocked. Then, while I was waiting for the door to open, this funny thing happened. I remembered I had the key in my pocket all the time, ha, ha! So I came in to tell you not to bother to let me in because I'd found the key after all.

MRS: So you went out again.

PRINGLE: No, no. It started to rain, and since I'd forgotten to put on my outdoor shoes I thought I'd not go for a walk this evening after all.

MRS: What a shame!

PRINGLE: Well, well. I went for a walk yesterday evening, when all's said and done. I dont't like to get into habits. [*He puts the lead on the table.*] In any case, Fido is not really fond of walking, you know [*He sits down in his chair.*] Not since she died . . .

[*He shakes his head sadly, and goes over to stand behind* MRS PRINGLE'S *chair. After a moment she stops knitting.*]

MRS: Ernest.

PRINGLE: Yes, dear.

MRS: What are you doing?

PRINGLE: Standing behind your chair, my dear.

MRS [*knitting*]: In all these years I have never known him to stand behind my chair. Why should he do so tonight . . . Is he going to kill me? Dear God, shall I scream? Shall I fall to my knees, bare my breast to his knife and implore his forgiveness? No, better not. I may be wrong. After all, I was wrong yesterday.

[*She continues knitting.*]

PRINGLE: Coming back to the subject of Fred . . .

MRS: Yes, dear.

PRINGLE: Taking it all in all, and making all due allowances, I still think it is fair to say that Fred was not blessed with what one might call a sense of humour.

MRS: He was a person of extreme breeding. He spoke French,

Italian and another language which I forget. English, that was it. Not only that, but he also had his own microscope. What ever you say about him, you must allow that. One has to go a long way nowadays to find a man who keeps his own microscopes.

PRINGLE: But, Ethel, I quite agree. All I say is—

MRS: I will not have you make a mockery of Fred.

PRINGLE: Ethel, really . . .

MRS: A is A and B is B and that's all there is to it.

PRINGLE: Very well, if that's the complexion you wish to put on it, I shall say no more about it. I shall not mention it again. My lips are sealed. The subject is closed. Very well. Enough.

[*He knocks his pipe out noisily and sits down.* MRS PRINGLE *knits. There is a pause.*]

MRS: If he had any weakness at all it was this: that he was not blessed with what you might call a sense of humour.

PRINGLE [*thoughtfully*]: Oh, I don't know. After all to be cut in half is no joke. I mean if *you're* the one who's cut in half. Of course, if you're someone else it might strike you differently, but if you're the *one* who's cut in half it would strike you differently. What I'm getting at is this: that after all, to be cut in half is no joke . . .

MRS: But, Ernest, even *before* he was cut in half he still hadn't what you might call a sense of humour.

PRINGLE: Hm?

MRS: *Before* . . .

PRINGLE: Before he was cut in half . . .

MRS: Yes.

PRINGLE: Hm . . . well yes . . . Now *before*, that's another matter.

MRS: I mean . . .

PRINGLE: Yes, yes, I see your point. You mean that even if he had *not* been cut in half he would still not have been blessed with what you might call a sense of humour?

MRS: Well, after all . . .

PRINGLE: You know, I believe that is true.

MRS: So it really makes no difference whether he was cut in half or not.

PRINGLE: That's one way of looking at it, certainly. You know, I think I shall have to think about that for a day or two. It's an idea that needs to grow in one's mind before one can appreciate it's full complexity . . . [*he sits back and closes his eyes.*]

MRS [*knitting*]: The nights are drawing in nicely . . . Or is it out? One of the two . . . Before long it will be winter again; or summer, whichever is due. Ho hum . . . Two purl, one plain as far as the armpit, then continue as below for six hundred and ninety-eight rows, casting off one stitch every seventh row or so, etc . . . It might have been better in a kind of green. But then again it might not. Nothing is certain until it's finished and done with. That much is certain . . .

[PRINGLE *snores suddenly, which wakes him. He jerks up.*]

PRINGLE: What the devil was that?

MRS: You snored, Ernest.

PRINGLE: Snored? But I'm awake.

MRS: Yes, dear.

PRINGLE: One can't turn one's back for a moment . . . [*he subsides into sleep again.*]

MRS: Oh, to be able to sleep as my husband does! Never a dull moment. Twenty-five years without a wink of sleep is more than a joke, in spite of the knitting one accomplishes in the meantime . . . There he sits with his eyes closed and the air whistling in and out of him. I'm sure I don't know what to make of it . . . I mean, where is he? I mean . . . Where is he? Ernest, where are you? [*No answer.*] No answer, you see . . . I could do whatever I liked now, and Ernest would never know, as long as I kept quiet about it. If only there was something I wanted to do . . . Cast off one stitch and continue . . .

What shall I do? Shall I swear softly? Good heavens, I know what I could do. I could dance in front of his chair with all my clothes off. *Really* all. What a terrifying sensation. If he opened his eyes, what would he do then? Close them again and pretend he was still asleep . . .? Oh God! Suppose he *didn't* close his eyes again, but instead took all his own clothes off and joined me! Suppose . . .

PRINGLE: A thought has just struck me. [*He sits up.*]

MRS: Ah . . . ! [*She covers her imaginary nakedness with her knitting.*]

PRINGLE: *If*, as we have agreed, Fred was not blessed with a sense of humour even before he was cut in half, then how was it that he became cut in half in the first place. Answer me that.

MRS: But, Ernest . . .

PRINGLE: Wait! My leg has gone to sleep. [*He stands up and stamps.*] One thing I thank God for. . .We live in a detached house. If my leg goes to sleep I am at liberty to stamp my foot as much as I please without fear of offending the neighbours. Also I can, if and when the fancy takes me, knock out my pipe on any of the four walls of this room. Freedom is a wonderful thing . . . The house in which Fred lived, on the other hand, was only semi-detached. Fred was able to knock out his pipe on only *three* walls.

MRS: But, Ernest . . .

PRINGLE: That isn't freedom. I don't care what anybody says.

MRS: But, Ernest . . .

PRINGLE: Three-quarter freedom, if you like, but not freedom.

MRS: But, Ernest, Fred smoked cigarettes.

PRINGLE: Exactly. Precisely. He dare not smoke a pipe for fear of the consequences. With a detached house it's quite different. I smoke what I please. Not cigars or cigarettes, of course, because of my chest. But anything else. A pipe . . .

MRS: Ernest, where are you when you're asleep?

PRINGLE: Is it a conundrum?

MRS: No, Ernest, I mean, where *are* you when you're asleep.
PRINGLE: In bed.

[*There is a pause.*]

Now let me elucidate my point.
MRS: Oh God . . . !
PRINGLE: The point is this: Fred, we agree, had no sense of humour. Yet Fred managed to get himself cut in half. Now, how was that?
MRS: How, Ernest?
PRINGLE: Yes, how?
MRS: But, Ernest, you did it yourself.
PRINGLE: My dear Ethel, I realise that. That is not the point at issue. The question is, *why* did I cut Fred in half?
MRS: Why.
PRINGLE: Yes, *why*. That is the question. Not whether. But *why*. After all, one doesn't do these things for no reason. Let us be logical. Why, that's the question. [*He yawns, returns to his seat, puts his head back and closes his eyes.*] Yes, yes a cup of tea and a cheese sandwich would be very nice. Or perhaps a cup of cocoa and beef dripping sandwich with salt and pepper. Beef dripping is nothing without salt and pepper. So my father used to say . . .
MRS: My father used to say the opposite.
PRINGLE: Really?
MRS: My father used to say that salt and pepper were nothing without beef dripping.
PRINGLE: It takes all sorts to make a world.
MRS: As to *why* you cut Fred in half . . .

[PRINGLE *sits up. There is a pause.*]

All I can say is, there must have been a reason for it.
PRINGLE: Exactly. Precisely.
MRS: He was an upright and God-fearing man.

PRINGLE: Agreed. My point, the very crux of my argument. What possible reason could there be to cut an honest and God-fearing man in half without so much as a by-your-leave, assuming that he had not what you might call a sense of humour...

MRS: But, Ernest...

PRINGLE: Allow me to continue. Now if he *had* had a sense of humour . . . he might have been *laughing* at me for some reason, and in *that* case I *might* have cut him in half.

MRS: Do you think so?

PRINGLE: Good gracious me, Yes. Might, you understand. Not necessarily would. Might. I do so hate being laughed at.

MRS: But, Ernest, Fred never laughed.

PRINGLE: Exactly. Precisely. Because he hadn't what you might call a sense of humour. But why, in that case, did I cut him in half?... It's a mystery. That's all I can say...

[*There is a pause.*]

MRS: Though, of course, seeing you in the wardrobe.

[*There is a pause.* PRINGLE *looks up.*]

PRINGLE: My dear Ethel, we are not talking of wardrobes. Wardrobes don't enter into the discussion.

MRS: No. Ernest... Except that seeing you in the wardrobe...

PRINGLE: Ethel, wardrobes are irrelevant!

[*There is a pause.*]

MRS: But seeing you in the wardrobe...

PRINGLE [*springing up*]: You are deliberately trying to goad me into an argument!

[*There is a pause.* PRINGLE *sits down again and glares at his wife. But she is knitting. He puts his head back, and closes his eyes. There is silence.*]

MRS: Cast off one stitch and continue . . . [*She does so. There is further silence.*]

PRINGLE: As for *in* the wardrobe . . .

[MRS PRINGLE *continues to knit.*]

It's absolutely preposterous . . . My dear Ethel, I have never been in a wardrobe in my life . . . Good gracious me, what do you take me for?

MRS: But Ernest, that's just it.

PRINGLE: What?

MRS: It was *on account of* Fred, you see.

PRINGLE: On account? . . . of Fred?

MRS: Continue for six rows, one purl, two plain, etc.

PRINGLE: I don't understand.

[*She knits.*]

Ethel, I don't understand . . .

[*She knits.*]

PRINGLE: Ethel!

MRS: On *account* of Fred, Ernest.

PRINGLE: On account of Fred I was in my wardrobe?

MRS: Not yours, Ernest.

PRINGLE: What?

MRS: Fred's.

PRINGLE: What?

MRS: Wardrobe.

PRINGLE: I was in *Fred's* wardrobe?

MRS: Yes, Ernest.

PRINGLE: Indeed. And what, may I ask, was I doing in Fred's wardrobe? Playing cricket, perhaps, or mountaineering? Or was I perhaps writing my memoirs? Eh?

MRS: No, Ernest.

PRINGLE: You're quite sure of that, Ethel? You're quite certain I wasn't playing cricket in the wardrobe? Now think carefully.

MRS: No, Ernest.

PRINGLE: Or lacrosse, perhaps. Lacrosse, was it? Ha, ha!

MRS: No, Ernest.

PRINGLE: Or polo, eh? [*He is highly amused.*] Polo, was I playing polo in the wardrobe? Eh! Eh?

MRS: Oh God!

PRINGLE: Not polo? You're certain I was not playing polo?

MRS: Ernest, you are destroying me.

PRINGLE: Then what, pray *was* I doing?

MRS: Hiding, Ernest.

PRINGLE: Hiding?

MRS: Yes, Ernest.

PRINGLE: From whom?

MRS: Fred.

PRINGLE: Hiding from Fred?

MRS: Would you like a cup of milky coffee?

PRINGLE: You may correct me if I am wrong. Perhaps I am labouring under a misapprehension as to this subject. But it seems to me that if I had wished to hide from Fred I should hide not in his wardrobe, but in my own.

MRS: But no, Ernest.

[MRS PRINGLE *knits.* PRINGLE *stands helplessly for a moment. Then he returns to his chair.*]

At that time, of course, you had no wardrobe of your own.

PRINGLE: I?

MRS: In any case.

PRINGLE: But, Ethel, I've always had a wardrobe.

MRS: No, Ernest.

PRINGLE: Not *always* of course. Naturally. I don't mean *always.* But in a manner of speaking, always. That is to say, nearly always. Certainly I've *nearly* always had a wardrobe of my own. Which is more than could be said for Fred.

MRS: But, Ernest . . .

PRINGLE: *Fred* didn't nearly always have a wardrobe of his own.

MRS: But, Ernest, Fred nearly *always* had a wardrobe of his own.

PRINGLE: A *dresser*. He nearly always had a *dresser* of his own.

MRS: He nearly always had a wardrobe of his own too.

PRINGLE: Are you sure?

MRS: Yes, Ernest.

PRINGLE: Well, I never . . . Do you know, all these years I've been thinking: whatever one says about Fred, this much is certain; he didn't nearly always have a wardrobe of his own. It just goes to show how you can think one thing and then think another.

MRS: There you are.

PRINGLE: Yes, indeed . . . So it was *Fred's* wardrobe I was hiding in! Well, I never.

[*There is a pause.*]

I wonder whatever became of that wardrobe.

MRS: But, Ernest . . . [*She looks at him.*]

PRINGLE: Hm?

MRS: But, Ernest it's upstairs.

PRINGLE: Upstairs?

MRS: Yes, Ernest.

PRINGLE: But there's no wardrobe upstairs. That is to say, there's *my* wardrobe upstairs. Not Fred's wardrobe.

MRS: But, Ernest . . .

PRINGLE: No, no, Ethel, you must give me right of way here. The wardrobe upstairs is *mine*. Not Fred's.

MRS: But it *was*.

PRINGLE: What?

MRS: The wardrobe.

PRINGLE: What?

MRS: Fred's, Ernest.

PRINGLE: My wardrobe was Fred's? Ethel, what are you saying?

MRS: It was Fred's.

PRINGLE: But, Ethel, I've nearly always had that wardrobe. Do you mean to tell me that *Fred* gave me that wardrobe?

MRS: Not exactly gave, Ernest.

PRINGLE: Then what?

MRS: He was cut in half, you see.

PRINGLE: What of it?

MRS: It was *after* he was cut in half.

PRINGLE: That he gave me the wardrobe.

MRS: Not exactly gave.

PRINGLE: Ah. Yes. Wait. I have it. Not *gave*. Took. Took. I took—

MRS: Not exactly *took*, Ernest.

PRINGLE: Yes, yes, took. I was hiding in Fred's wardrobe. *Then* I cut him in half. *Then* I took his wardrobe. Good gracious me, is *that* why I cut him in half? To take his wardrobe?

MRS: Not exactly take, Ernest.

PRINGLE: My dear Ethel . . . Fred had a wardrobe. I cut Fred in half. The wardrobe is upstairs. Very well. *Who took the wardrobe?*

MRS: No one took it, Ernest. It stayed there.

PRINGLE: Ethel, I don't think you quite follow my line of reasoning. Fred had a wardrobe . . . In his house . . .

MRS: But, Ernest, this *was* Fred's house.

PRINGLE: But this is *my* house!

MRS: Yes, Ernest, but it *was* Fred's house.

[PRINGLE *gets up, goes over to the corner of the room, and examines the room.*]

PRINGLE: But, Ethel, I've nearly always had this house.

MRS: Nearly always is not always.

PRINGLE: Are you sure it was . . . ?

MRS: Yes, Ernest.

PRINGLE: Then I'll tell you what this does. It puts a new light on things. It makes the whole situation appear as a horse of a completely different complexion. Now, let me recapitulate: I was in Fred's wardrobe, hiding. From Fred, from Fred, was it?

[MRS PRINGLE *knits*.]

I then cut him in half . . . By the way, did we agree that Fred had a moustache, or no moustache?

[MRS PRINGLE *knits*.]

I want to get a mental picture, you understand. I wish to see it with my mind's eye . . . Now: I am in the wardrobe, I am hiding from Fred. Suddenly . . . Wait!

[MRS PRINGLE *looks up then continues knitting*.]

PRINGLE: Yes, this could be it. This could be the solution to the whole problem! [*He puts his glasses on*.] Listen! The reason I cut Fred in half was: that he *discovered* where I was hiding! Ha? Ha? [*He looks triumphantly at* MRS PRINGLE, *who knits. He sits down and sleeps*.]

MRS: Cast off fourteen stitches working from the neck backwards alternately, purl, plain, and so on. Gents move to the centre, salute your partner and away we go. [*She knits*.] There he goes again. In goes the air through his nose; out it comes again through his mouth. You'd hardly think it was worth it . . . Fred, now, was exceptional. Fred breathed *in* through his mouth and *out* through his nose. Fred was a person of will-power. Breathing in through his mouth and out through his nose stopped him from dreaming. Or made him dream, one of the two. The main thing, of course, was that he was in control of himself . . . Daddy once said gentlemen dream about all sorts of things. But all Ernest ever dreams about is a wall. A wall. All night he dreams about this wall. As soon as he drops off to sleep he begins to dream about the wall, and he dreams about it until he wakes up again. He must be doing it now. He says it is a most vivid dream. Here is this wall in front of him he says, so long that he can't see the end of it, and so high that he can't see either its top or its bottom. Not a brick wall, you understand. Just a plain *wall*. Flat. Not shiny. Just flat and plain, no top, no bottom, no sides . . . Ernest says that if he didn't *know* it was a wall, he wouldn't know it *was* a wall. But he's quite sure, it is a wall. I say: But, Ernest, how do you *know* it's a wall? And he says: I *know* it's a wall. And I say: But how do you *know* it's a wall? And he says: What else could it be? Good gracious me, he says, after dreaming about the same wall eight hours a night all my life I think I should know whether it's a wall or not. And I say: But suppose it isn't a wall, suppose it isn't *anything*, suppose it's *nothing*, and you only *think* it's a wall. And he says: Are you trying to tell me I've been dreaming about nothing all my life? And thinking it was a wall? And I say: Really, Ernest, I don't know, and he says: In any case, the proof is that it's flat. Like a wall. Flat. How can *nothing* be flat? And I say: But, Ernest, how do you *know* that it's flat? And he says: My dear Ethel, I can *see* it's flat. And I say: But if it hasn't any colour and you can't see the ends of it or the top or bottom how do you *know*? But he insists it's a wall. He won't have it any other way. Every morning up he wakes and says: Ethel, guess what I dreamed about last night? And I say, no. And he says: A *wall*. He is not what you might call a person of great imagination . . . His father also, dreamt about a wall. It runs in the family . . . As to whether it was the *same* wall, that's another matter.

[*She knits. Suddenly* PRINGLE *sits bolt upright.*]

PRINGLE: What was that?
MRS: Nothing, Ernest.
PRINGLE: Well, well . . . Do you know, I had a most vivid dream.

MRS: A wall?
PRINGLE: Two walls. One behind the other . . .

[MRS PRINGLE *knits*.]

This, then, as I see it, is the picture. I am hiding in the wardrobe. Enter Fred. He looks around. I am not to be seen. Strange. Where am I? I must be somewhere (and indeed I am, Ethel. I am, in reality, in the wardrobe. But of this, you understand, Fred is unaware). He looks around. Where can I be?
MRS: In the wardrobe.
PRINGLE: Yes, yes, Ethel, the question is rhetorical. It does not require an answer. A figure of speech you understand . . . He looks around. Where can I be?
MRS: In the wardrobe.

[PRINGLE *gets up in a huff, takes up the dog's lead and opens the door*.]

PRINGLE: I am going to take the dog for a walk!
MRS: But, Ernest, you already have.
PRINGLE: Then I shall take the cat for a walk!
MRS: The cat died, Ernest.
PRINGLE: Poor Fred. Tck tck tck . . .
MRS: To go to Church regularly every Christmas Day, and then be cut in half. It doesn't seem right. If it had been in quarters, now. That would be different. Or eighths. Or sixteenths. Or thirty-seconds. Or sixty-fourths. Or hundred and . . .
PRINGLE: It all comes to the same . . . You see, Ethel, this is the way I see it: if he'd *laughed* when he found me in his wardrobe. If he'd seen the funny side of it, it would have turned out quite differently. If he'd just *smiled* . . . It wasn't as though he *knew* he was going to be cut in half.
MRS: That's true.

PRINGLE: He should have laughed. It was only decent. I would
have laughed. If I found someone hiding in my wardrobe, I'd
laugh. Wouldn't you laugh?

MRS: I suppose so.

PRINGLE: Only one thing puzzles me, Ethel, when I hid in Fred's
wardrobe and then Fred came in and found me and I cut him
in half... Where were you?

MRS: In bed, Ernest.

PRINGLE: In bed?

MRS: Yes, Ernest.

PRINGLE: But, Ethel, I *always* go to bed before you. If *you* were in
bed, how is it that *I* was in the wardrobe?

MRS: You got up again, Ernest.

PRINGLE: Up? I?

MRS: Yes, Ernest.

PRINGLE: But I never get up again.

MRS: You did this time.

PRINGLE: Why?

MRS: To hide in the wardrobe.

PRINGLE: Now wait. Wait, there's a flaw in the logic of this somewhere. There's a discrepancy. Listen. Let me set the scene. You
were in bed. Correct?

MRS: Yes.

PRINGLE: I also was in bed... The same bed?

MRS: Yes.

PRINGLE: Now: I got out of bed. I hid in the wardrobe. Fred
found me in the wardrobe. You were in bed. Hm?

MRS: Yes, Ernest.

PRINGLE: Very well. Now. Answer me this. Who let Fred in?

MRS: But, Ernest...

PRINGLE: You were in bed. I was in the wardrobe...

MRS: But he let himself in.

PRINGLE: Self.

MRS: It was his house.

PRINGLE: Oh. Ah. Yes. Hm . . . No, wait!!! Ethel, what are you saying?

MRS: Would you care for a glass of hot milk?

PRINGLE: If it was *Fred's* house, Ethel, what were *we* doing in bed in it?

[MRS PRINGLE *puts down her knitting. They look at each other. There is a long pregnant pause.*]

MRS: Perhaps we were tired, Ernest.

PRINGLE: No, Ethel, I can't have that. Because if we were tired, why didn't we go *home* to bed?

MRS: But, Ernest, I *was* at home.

PRINGLE: Ethel, you don't seem to understand the situation. This was *Fred's* house. We've arrived at that. It was *Fred's* house . . .

MRS: I realise that, Ernest.

PRINGLE: Well, then, how can you say . . . ?

MRS: But Ernest, I was Fred's wife.

PRINGLE: Fred's . . . But, Ethel . . . But you're *my* wife, Ethel. You're married to me. I'm almost *certain* of that. You've nearly *always* been married to me.

MRS: Nearly always is not always, Ernest.

PRINGLE: But if you . . . But, Ethel, if you . . .

[*There is a pause.*]

But if you were *Fred's* wife, what were *we* . . . ? [*He sits forward, hand on chin. He gets up, looks at* MRS PRINGLE, *begins to pace slowly to and fro, stops, looks at* MRS PRINGLE, *paces to and fro; stops, and is lost in thought. There is a pause.*]

MRS: We were lovers . . . We were lovers, Ernest . . .

[*Ernest is engrossed in his meditation.*]

Ernest, we were lovers! Lovers! Lovers!!!!

[*She knits quietly.* PRINGLE *is unheeding; presently she stops knitting.*]

How is it I wonder, that one can be one thing, and then be a completely different thing?

[PRINGLE *returns to his chair.*]

PRINGLE: Well, well, well, it's all a mystery. That's all I can say. That's my honest opinion. A mystery . . .

[*But* MRS PRINGLE *now is gazing into space.*]

And another funny thing is this: how is it that, if our house is detached, Fred's house was only semi-detached? When they're one and the same house? Now that bears thinking about, Ethel. It bears thinking about . . . Yes, yes, why not. And a cheese sandwich perhaps. That would be very nice . . . [*He rests his head back and closes his eyes.*]

RETURN TO A CITY

First performance at the Questors Theatre, Ealing, June 1960

WOMAN	Patricia Hooper
1ST MAN	Laurence Nixon
2ND MAN	Peter Browning
GIRL	Barbara Jackson
TRAVELLER	Victor Pompini

Directed by PETER WHELAN

CHARACTERS
in order of appearance

WOMAN

1ST MAN

2ND MAN

GIRL

TRAVELLER

RETURN TO A CITY

[*What was once the drawing-room of what was once a house. It has the appearance to be expected of a room which has been open, via wall and roof, to the weather for many years. The furniture is sticks and stones.*
Beyond what were once the french windows is a suggestion of ruins. At them, stands a woman, who is in her fifties at least. She is calling her dog. In her hand is a bone.]

WOMAN: Nemmy . . . Nemmy . . . Nemmy . . .

[*The dog growls.*]

I thought you'd gone for good at last, and left me on my own. Not that you're much company.

[*The dog growls.*]

Don't you bare your teeth at me. I know you'd like to eat me, but you can't, can you? Here. I've saved you a nice big bone as a special treat. There . . .

[*She throws the bone down. The dog eats.*]

Is it a nice boney, the? . . .

[*The dog growls. The woman sings to herself.*]

> Bye, Baby Bunting,
> Daddy's gone a-hunting,
> To find a little . . .

You stay away for days on end, and when you decide to come home there's a bone waiting for you. Why do I do it? to stop you from eating me up? . . . I was keeping that bone for the master. Never mind, if he doesn't bring something in we'll just have to stay hungry, won't we? . . .

> To find a little bunny skin
> To wrap my Baby Bunting in.
> Bye...

Eaten it all? Come here and be nursed, then . . . Nemmy, come back, don't leave me alone. Stay with me for a . . . No, why should you. After all, it's a free . . .

[*There is silence.*]

> To find a little nourishment
> To save us from our punishment.
> Bye, Baby...

[*Silence.*]

Listen . . . Listen . . . Nothing. No sound . . . Nothing . . . Bye . . . Babe . . .

[*Silence.*]

I must clean the walls. That's what I'll do. I wonder I didn't think of it before. I should have done it long ago, I can see that now . . . Dirty, they are. I must get to straight away. Where did I put that brush? . . . Not here . . . Ah!

[*She finds the remains of a long-handled brush.*]

I'll begin here. Then I'll go back and see if I can see any difference.

[*She scrubs for a moment.*]

Now...

[*She goes to the far side of the room.*]

Well, yes . . . Oh, yes. Different altogether. I really think this will make the room look *bigger*.

[*She goes back, raises the brush and pauses.*]

Do I want the room bigger? . . . But in any case it'll get dirty again.

[*She scrubs, then stops.*]

There were noises once. Not noises, noise, a continuous noise, of one kind or another. Wasn't there?

[*She scrubs a moment, then stops.*]

You start to scrub a wall, the noise of it fills your ears, and then you stop . . . and there's nothing. No sound . . . But there *were* sounds once. What? . . . Trees? Why trees? Trees had no voices. No legs either. No, wait, wait. *Leaves.* Each tree carried many branches, and each branch—twig, and each twig, *leaves.* The effect was of a sack covering the bones of the tree, but a sack hung by a single thread. A slight wind had the effect of *moving* the leaves, and the thousands of leaves each rubbing and slapping against its neighbour produced—a sound.
Sssssss .sssssssssh . . .
It would be nice to have a tree . . .
My word, that must have been a sound.
Ssssssss . . . . sssssssh . . .

[*She stops. There is silence.*]

[*Out of doors. Two men are walking slowly over the rocks. They are in their fifties.*]

1ST MAN: I tell you it's true.
2ND MAN: So you say.
1ST: So I say, so I say. I say it because it's true. Why else should I say it? Answer me that. Why should I say it if it isn't true?
2ND: I'm not saying it's not true.
1ST: Then what are you saying?

[*They stop walking.*]

Well?

2ND: I'm not saying anything. You're saying. You're saying something's true. I'm not arguing.

1ST: But you disbelieve me.

2ND: I don't disbelieve you.

1ST: Then you believe me. Answer me.

2ND: I must get home. My wife has a bone.

[*He makes to walk off. The other stops him.*]

1ST: Either you believe me or you don't believe me!

2ND: Not necessarily . . .

1ST: Then what? Answer me that!

2ND: What do you mean, then what?

1ST: If you neither believe me nor disbelieve me, then what?

2ND: Nothing.

1ST: Nothing?

2ND: Nothing, my dear fellow, Nothing. Nothing . . . Nothing! Nothing!! Can I make it any plainer!! . . .

[*He sits down.*]

2ND: My feet ache. I think. I may be mistaken . . .

[*His companion also sits, on an adjacent bit of rock.*]

On my feet since dawn, walking, hunting, walking, in no great discomfort. Then I stop walking, start talking, and my feet ache.

[*He looks at his companion.*]

I try to avoid this kind of thing.

1ST: Don't you care?

2ND: They can ache if they want to.

1ST: Not your feet. What I told you.

2ND: What was that?

1ST: The prisoners! I met someone who knew someone who *saw* them! Well?

2ND: So you say.

1ST: How can you deny it!

2ND: So you say so he says. So he says. What do you expect of me?

1ST: Will you assume the possibility?

2ND: If you like.

1ST: Very well. That's all I ask . . .

[*A pause.*]

2ND: Do you want a cigarette?

1ST: You haven't *got* any.

[*The* 2ND MAN *produces a packet of cigarettes.*]

My dear chap . . .

2ND: Observe. . .

[*He holds up the packet.*]

A transparent cover . . .

[*He removes it.*]

A cardboard cover.

[*He taps it with his finger, and opens it.*]

A metallic cover.

[*He removes the foil and smells the cigarettes. He passes the packet to the* 1ST MAN, *who also smells them.*]

1ST: Not very stale at all. Where did you . . . ?

2ND: Found them.

1ST: Three covers. The complexity of it . . .

[*He offers the packet back.*]

2ND: Take one.

1ST: No, no. You take the first.

[*The* 2ND MAN *accepts the packet, takes out two cigarettes, puts the packet away, and gives one of the cigarettes to his friend, who examines it, smells it, then looks up at him with the gleeful chuckle of a child with a new toy. There is a pause.*]

Have you got a match?
2ND: A what?
1ST: Match.
2ND: No.
1ST: After all, one can't have everything . . .

[*He realises the joke, and begins to laugh.*]

Did you hear that? One can't have . . .

[*His laughter changes to sobbing. He stops.*]

[*There is a pause.*]

It'll get better. Sometimes I *feel* it. It'll get better.

[*There is a pause.*]

2ND: No . . .
1ST: No?
2ND: Let it lie . . .

[*A pause.*]

1ST: These prisoners.
2ND: My dear fellow . . .
1ST: Are you not interested in current affairs?

[*The other looks at him in surprise.*]

Do you not wish to know what's going on in the world? Have you no thought for the future?!

[*The* 2ND MAN *shakes in a peculiar way.*]

1ST: Are you ill?

2ND: Laughing...

[*He shakes.*]

1ST: Laughing?

2ND: You remind me of something.

1ST: What?

2ND: I forget. [*Shaking uncontrollably.*] I forget. I forget! [*Shaking*] Oh God! I forget...

[*The* 1ST MAN *stands up in a huff.*]

1ST: If you insist on approaching the situation in this frame of mind I think there's nothing more to be said. I shall make my way home. I am glad to have met you.

[*He begins to walk off, while the other continues to shake. He turns once, sees him still shaking...*]

It's people like you who've made the country what it is today.

[*He stalks off with dignity. The* 2ND MAN *is convulsed. He puts his hands to the sides of his face and, doubled up, shakes. After a while he subsides. He stands upright, and looks in the direction the other has taken. He speaks in a normal voice.*]

2ND: You ask whether I have any thought of the future... My dear fellow. My dear, dear fellow, I am full of thoughts for the future. I am a mass of apprehensions. What do you expect of me? Each time I breathe... My dear fellow, each time my lungs collapse I find myself thinking; very well; after this it will be necessary to fill them up again. If possible. Unless I stop, unless I forget, unless I choose not to, unless I—resign. Who drives my heart, tell me that? I From second to second. Come along, heart. I say, just another beat or two and no questions asked, just another beat or two come what may, and then another, and one more, and again, and a few more after that, and another and another and another and another and so on and so on and so on and so on and so on! Thought for the future, my dear fellow! Who do you think holds me in the vertical position? *I. My* muscles. I work them I tell them to hold on, from minute to minute, from second to second, year in and year out. *I* do it. Look at me! All in one piece. You talk to me about the future! Look at me. Don't you see? *I* am standing *upright* on the ends of my legs, holding my mind inside my body! The future? Ha! My dear fellow, the future is this: My wife . . . has a *bone* for me! My wife has a bone for me!! My wife has a bone for me!! For that future I shall perform the feat of walking home, balanced on the ends of my legs without once touching the ground with my fingers! What more do you want! Tell me that! What more do you want? ! ! !...

[*In the silence that follows he becomes aware of himself again; looks down the length of his body at his feet, as though from a great height, stands erect again, turns aimlessly round and begins to walk off. The* 1ST MAN *comes back and catches him up. He looks round and stops walking.*]

1ST: It's all right for you. You've got a wife waiting for you . . . I'm a bachelor . . . We all have our differences of opinion. Do you ever dream you're a dog?

[*The* 2ND MAN *makes no response.*]

I do. It recurs. I wake up in a quandary. I think: should I stand up on two legs or on all fours? Which is right. But dogs can't talk, you see. Dogs can't engage in argument . . .

2ND: I must get home. My wife . . .

[*He is walking off. The other follows him.*]

1ST: I'm going that way.

[*The* 2ND MAN *looks at him.*]

Am I not?

[*He points to his feet, and laughs delightedly.*]

Am I not?

[*He laughs again.*]

You see the joke?

[*He points to his feet, clasping the* 2ND MAN *round the shoulder.*]

It's my feet. You see? Ha. Ha. None of my business. Ha ha ha.
There they go. After them, after them. Ha ha ha . . .

[*They walk off.*]

[*A line of men walking in double file. A background of grass-covered
hills. The men walk slowly, as though weighed down with chains.
The sun is setting. At the end of the line is a man, in his late thirties
like the rest of them, with a* GIRL *of about sixteen by his side. This
last* TRAVELLER *stops suddenly. The rest do not notice, but the* GIRL,
after a pace, stops and looks back at him. The TRAVELLER *is looking
over to his right.*]

GIRL: What's the matter?
TRAVELLER: Nothing's the matter. We go this way.
GIRL: But what about the others?
TRAVELLER: What about them?
GIRL: Aren't you going to say goodbye? After coming all this
way with them?

[*He looks past her at the retreating line of men.*]

TRAVELLER: What's the use of saying goodbye? They've served
their purpose.
GIRL: I don't understand.
TRAVELLER: Forget it.
GIRL: The sun's setting.
TRAVELLER: It happens every day.

GIRL: It'll be dark soon. And we'll be alone.

TRAVELLER: What did you expect? . . . If you don't like the idea, go with them.

GIRL: Would you let me?

TRAVELLER: No.

[*He holds out his hand. She looks at him, hesitates, looks again at the line of men, then back at him; then she runs to him and clasps his arm with both hers. They begin walking.*]

GIRL: How can you tell this is the way?

TRAVELLER: I can tell.

GIRL: But there's nothing to see. How can you tell?

TRAVELLER: Why do you ask so many damned questions?

GIRL: You *know* why. Because I know nothing! How can I learn if I don't ask?

[*She stops suddenly, holding his arm.*]

Listen: I've thought of something.

TRAVELLER: Keep it.

GIRL: No Listen. I was alone. That's right, isn't it? I was quite alone. Eating and sleeping, like an animal.

TRAVELLER: That's over. Forget it.

GIRL: But it didn't seem wrong. I hadn't learnt to think. You were the first people I'd ever seen. I crouched in my hiding place and watched you lighting a fire, making noises to each other; when you found me and grabbed me by the wrists and pulled me into the firelight, I just crouched at your feet and shook and shook. I suddenly saw that you were all wearing clothes on your bodies, and I had nothing. I crouched there and waited to be eaten.

[*He laughs.*]

Then another man tried to grab hold of me, and you killed him. Those are the first things I remember. And yet the

strange thing is, I didn't want to run away. It was almost as
though I wanted to be eaten.

TRAVELLER: You had the wrong idea.

GIRL: But wait a minute, this is what I wanted to say: I knew
nothing when you took me. I was an animal. Everything I
know I know from you. Talking, mating, thinking ... You've
made me, haven't you? Out of nothing. And if you're
wrong ...

TRAVELLER: Wrong?

GIRL: What do I mean? . . . You made me, so if you're . . .
wrong ... If there's another ... possibility ... No, don't hurt
me. I must ask this!

TRAVELLER: It's getting late.

GIRL: Listen! If *someone else* had found me. Not you, Someone
else ...

TRAVELLER: Be quiet! ... You know nothing.

GIRL: But ...

TRAVELLER: *I* found you.

GIRL: Yes.

[*Clinging to his arm with both hers, she walks on.*]

[*The* 1ST *and* 2ND MAN, *walking.*]

1ST: . . . the situation is fluid. That's my philosophy, and alway
has been. The situation is fluid, in spite of appearances. One
has to take the broad view. Perspective is the thing, a sense of
perspective. Defeatism is barren; optimism is the correct note,
realistic optimism. Tempered with caution, of course. Kept in
perspective, naturally. Progress is inevitable. Victory is
assured. We shall win through ...

[*The* 2ND MAN *stops walking. The* 1ST MAN *also stops. The* 2ND
MAN *sits down and takes off his shoe—or begins to, then realises he is
not wearing any. He begins to shake.*]

Don't you agree?

[*The* 2ND MAN *shakes, his head in his hands.*]

Are you laughing?

[*The* 2ND MAN *shakes.*]

1ST: If you find me funny . . .
2ND: Not you, my dear fellow.
1ST: What, then?
2ND: I stopped to take off my shoe to remove a stone.
1ST [*looking at his feet*]: But . . .

[*The* 2ND MAN *begins to laugh again. The* 1ST MAN *also begins to laugh. He is overcome by the humour of it. Tears roll down his face.*]

2ND: I don't remember when I wore shoes . . .

[*He shakes violently again. The* 1ST MAN *is convulsed. He sits down. They subside.*]

Have another cigarette.
1ST: No thanks, I've still got the last one.

[*He produces it. They laugh again.*]

It'll last me a long time . . . It's indestructable . . So long . . .
So long as I can't . . . light it . . .

[*He is convulsed. The* 2ND MAN *rocks from side to side. The* 1ST MAN *raises his hand for silence, though only he, of course is making any noise.*]

Thus . . . Thus I also save *matches* . . .

[*He wipes his eyes. The* 2ND MAN *is in agony, holding his head in one hand and beating the ground with the other as he shakes. They subside.*]

1ST [*putting his hand on the other's shoulder*]: My dear friend, you don't know what company means to me . . .

[*The* 2ND MAN *begins to shake again.*]

I am a gregarious creature . . .

[*He stops as the other shakes more. The* 2ND MAN *looks round at him, and sweeps his hand round the devastated horizon.*]

I love crowds . . .

[*He is convulsed again. They subside.*]

2ND: You must stay the night with us.
1ST: No, really, I couldn't impose . . .
2ND: Not at all.
1ST: But your wife . . .
2ND: Delighted.
1ST: You're sure?
2ND: I insist.
1ST: That's most kind of you.
2ND: Of course, you must take us as you find us . . .
1ST [*in the spirit of it*]: I shall be charmed . . .
2ND: We have three walls.
1ST: Three, eh?
2ND: Nearly three.

[*They laugh.*]

Two and a bit . . . A little bit . . .
1ST: Roof?
2ND: Half a roof.
1ST: A whole half roof?
2ND: Half a whole roof.
1ST [*gasping*]: No! Chimney?
2ND [*seriously*]: Unfortunately, no . . .
1ST [*also serious*]: How sad.
2ND: But . . . [*shaking*] . . . the remains are clearly visible.

[*They laugh, and subside. The* 1ST MAN *shifts slightly, and looks at the ground between them.*]

1ST: Hullo, what's this?

[*He peers at an object just visible between the rocks. He seizes it and tries to move it.*]

2ND: It may go down any distance.
1ST: It moves.

[*He stands up and removes a piece of rock, takes a better hold on the bar and waggles it to and fro. It loosens. He pulls and frees it, and stands up holding it. It is a motor-car starting handle. They look at it, then at each other. The 1ST MAN looks again at the handle. The 2ND MAN begins to shake. The 1ST MAN looks up, and explodes into laughter.*]

2ND: Well, well ... Now you have it.
1ST: No, no, we both found it. *We* have it.
2ND: Really, I couldn't ...
1ST: I insist.
2ND: You are too kind.
1ST: Not at all ...

[*There is a pause while they savour the joke.*]

Would you care to examine it?
2ND: May I?
1ST: It's half yours.

[*He hands it to the other, who turns it over in his hands.*]

2ND: Most interesting.
1ST: Bent, you notice. Not just straight. Bent.
2ND: And not merely once. Twice. It's bent. Observe.
1ST: In two different directions. Complex ...
2ND: To say the least ...

[*They snigger.*]

And notice its prodigious capabilities. A straight rod . . .

[*running a finger along one of its straights*] A curved rod . . .
[*indicating its roundness*] A bent rod . . . [*indicating a bend.*]

1ST: Twice.
2ND: It stands . . . [*holding it vertically*] It lies . . . [*holding it
horizontally*] It sits . . . [*diagonally*] Crouches . . . Kneels . . .
1ST [*gasping*]: Such a rod!
2ND: My dear fellow—we are men of property.

[*The* 1ST MAN *stops laughing.*]

1ST: That's another way of looking at it. You know, this is a
serious thing.
2ND: Undoubtedly.
1ST: We own an object. An object, moreover, which probably
once had a use.
2ND: Quite probably.
1ST: Wait . . . Hold this end.

[*He does so.*]

Both hands.

[*He does so.*]

Are you ready? . . . Very well. Go . . .

[*He cranks the handle. After a moment the* 2ND MAN *begins to
shake. The* 1ST MAN *starts laughing again. Still turning the handle
he roars with laughter, while the other shakes tremendously. He
stops turning and they both give themselves over to their laughter,
which engulfs them, prostrates them, leaves the* 1ST MAN *sobbing
bitterly and the* 2ND *motionless except for an occasional heave, head
dropped onto his shoulders. They come to themselves, look at each
other and at the handle which the* 1ST MAN *is still holding. There is a
pause. The joke is over.*]

2ND: I must get home . . .

[*They look at each other. The* 1ST MAN *finds the handle in his hand, and throws it down.*]

1ST: It'll get better . . .

[*He looks sideways at the other, then down at his feet.*]

2ND: No . . .

[*The* 1ST MAN *looks at him again. There is a pause. The* 2ND MAN *begins to walk slowly in the direction they were going. As he reaches the fallen handle he stops, looks at it for a moment, then picks it up and hurls it with all his force at the ground again. He picks up a rock in both hands, holds it above his head, and is about to pound it on to the handle. His head drops, he lowers the rock to the ground and walks slowly off followed by the* 1ST MAN.]

No . . .

[*A slight rise. The* TRAVELLER *and the* GIRL *are sitting on the ground, resting. The man is looking across the country; the* GIRL, *as usual, is looking at him. They are silent.*]

GIRL: Have you any bread?

[*He produces some, breaks it in two and gives her half. They eat, he looking across country, she watching him. She turns her head and looks in the direction he is looking.*]

What can you see? . . . Stones? You don't look as though you're looking at stones. But that's all I can see, as far as I can see, just a lot of old stones. No sound. Nothing moving. Is that how you left it? Did you expect something else when you came back to it? . . . It's *nothing* is it? It's . . . stones . . . *You* lived *here*?

TRAVELLER: Me and ten million others.

GIRL: What is a million?

TRAVELLER: More than you can imagine.

GIRL: You all lived here?

TRAVELLER: Look out there: think of all that, covered with buildings; stone boxes, as far as you can see. But not dead; living shaking with life like a great stone animal. A city. Two hundred churches, three million houses, ten million people. You could hear its voice from here, a great throbbing roar. The sound of ten million people living their lives.

GIRL: What are churches?

TRAVELLER: Buildings! Buildings...

GIRL: But you knew it would be like this. Is this what you've come back for? After how many years? Explain to me ... [*suddenly angry*] Am I *so* ignorant? Fifteen years you waited to come back; so you told me. To *this*? These ... *stones* ... Why can't I see what you see!? What did you expect to find.

TRAVELLER: A rock pushed upright ... After fifteen years, they could have done *that* ...

GIRL: Who? ... You're crying ... What for? ... The stones? ... Is it the stones you're going back for?

TRAVELLER: Where else would you have me go?

GIRL: I wasn't unhappy before you found me ... Here, It's so still. So silent. I'm frightened. This isn't a good place. I don't want to go into it. There's something wrong, there's something ... It's not quite a sound. What is it? Can you hear it? Tell me what it is, it frightens me, it's something I don't understand. Teach me. How many people? How many people? Is that it? What is it? ... Explain to me ... !!

[*As she speaks the sound grows louder, the sound of the city. It rises to a crescendo, becoming suddenly a single person's scream—it may be the girl's—and then a sudden silence. She has thrown herself forward so that her head is on his lap, and is sobbing, clutching at him. He is still looking out over the city, tears on his face.*]

Explain to me ... Explain to me ...

[*He looks down at her head, and strokes her hair.*]

GIRL: What was it?

TRAVELLER: My memories. My memories . . .

[*She lifts her head and looks at him, not quite understanding.*]

GIRL: Will it happen again?

TRAVELLER: I don't know.

[*He gets to his feet, and helps her to hers.*]

Come on.

GIRL: Must we?

TRAVELLER: Yes.

[*He takes a few steps down the hill towards the city. He stops, and looks back as he did before. She stands looking at him.*]

Come on.

[*He turns, and continues walking. After a moment the GIRL runs down after him and puts her arm round his waist. He puts his arm on her shoulder, and they walk on.*]

[*The TWO MEN, walking.*]

1ST: After all . . . when all's said and done . . . life goes on . . .

[*The 2ND MAN stops walking, and looks at him expressionlessly. The 1ST MAN also stops.*]

Let us be frank with one another. Life goes on . . . Does it not? There's no denying it. Very well, then. We are in agreement on a fundamental point. Now, let us progress.

[*The 2ND MAN begins walking.*]

No, wait! I'm on the track of something.

[*The 2ND MAN stops.*]

2ND: My wife has a bone . . .

1ST: Bones are secondary.
2ND: To you. Not to me . . . And it's getting dark.
1ST: There's a moon.

[*The* 1ST MAN *sits down.*]

Now listen. This is my argument: Life goes on. On that we're agreed. Right. Now. What's the next step? One: it can get worse. Two: it can get better. Three: it can stay the same.

[*The* 2ND MAN *also sits down, and puts his head in his hands.*]

Now, let us take the possibilities one by one. First, if it gets worse . . . If it gets worse it gets worse. But *then*, it can either get worse, again, or get better, or stay the same. Life goes on. My dear chap, life goes on . . . Two. If it gets better it gets better. Good. Three. . . If it stays the same—it stays the same. The same.

[*The* 2ND MAN *looks up.*]

It stays the same. Life goes on . . .

[*The* 2ND MAN *is expressionless.*]

Don't you understand, are you a complete idiot! It stays the same, life goes on. Better, worse, it stays the same! Life goes on!!

[*There is a pause. The* 2ND MAN *is expressionless.*]

[*doubtfully*] Is there a flaw in the argument? . . . It stays the same . . .

[*There is a pause.*]

Listen, what do you expect? Nobody made any promises. Very well, then. Here we are, and that's that . . . You've got a roof over your head . . . Half a roof . . . You think things are bad. Well, then, tell me this: how do you know? How can you judge? Things might be good, for all you know. Or either.

Who are you to say? Your feet hurt, you say. Well, what about it? Are we to make judgment on the basis of how much your feet hurt? It's ridiculous. *My* feet don't hurt. Very well, whose feet are we to judge by?

2ND: My mind hurts . . .

1ST: Your what?

2ND: My mind hurts, my mind hurts, my mind hurts!

1ST: Where?

2ND: Where?

1ST: Where, where? In what region? Show me it . . . Where shall I apply the bandage? My dear chap, you are talking in the abstract. Mind? Which mind? Where is the mind?

2ND: My mind—

1ST: There is no mind. I see no mind . . .

[*There is a pause.*]

Very well. Supposing it does. What of it? Who are you? How much space do you take up? Wait, look, look at that rock. Look at it. It's about your size. It takes up as much space. Very well, what of the rock? Do its feet hurt? Hey, rock! Do your feet hurt? Your mind? . . . No answer. The rock is content. One for and one against. You see my argument. The logic is impregnable. One must be realistic, optimistically realistic. Life goes on. It comes to the—

2ND: My dear fellow!!

[*The* 1ST MAN *stops short in astonishment.*]

You miss the point. I think my feet ache, but they may not. I'm not dogmatic about it. I believe I feel cold, but it's quite possible I feel hot. I don't really care. Because I am at the moment obsessed with the idea of pushing myself over these stones to where *I think* I have a wife who I *think* has a bone for me . . . That's all. This is my life. My wife has a bone for me . . . Aching feet are a luxury, don't you understand!!

[*There is a pause. The* 2ND MAN *turns slowly and with great effort of will manages to get himself started in the direction in which he wants to go.*]

1ST: My dear friend, this is escapism.

[*The* 2ND MAN *stops. The* 1ST MAN *goes up to him.*]

One must face the facts. History is on our side . . . Listen. I *spoke* to a man who *spoke* to one of them.

[*The* 2ND MAN *looks slowly at him.*]

The prisoners, one of the prisoners, there's no doubt about it. They're coming back. Some of them. One or two. They'll know what to do. They have experience. They've travelled, my dear chap, that's what they've done. They'll have the answers. They'll know what to do. We only need a lead, that's all. Just to put ourselves in their hands.

[*The* 2ND MAN *has put his hands over his ears, turned again, and is walking slowly away, followed by the* 1ST MAN, *still talking . . .*]

[*The house, from outside. Moonlight. Some kind of light burning inside. The* WOMAN *is inside, singing.*]

WOMAN: Bye, Baby Bunting.
Daddy's gone a-hunting.
To find a little nourishment,
To save us from our punishment . . .

[*She is sitting looking down at the dog which dozes unseen at her feet. She stops singing suddenly. She looks up, listening. There is silence.*]

Nothing . . . No sound . . . You're only a dog, Nemmy. All you remember is stones and bones . . . But listen, Nemmy, I'll tell you a secret . . . [*whispering*] It wasn't always like this, I pretend it was but it wasn't. There were—*sounds*, Nemmy, the air was full of sounds, there was no escape from them. And people. *Multitudes.* The ground swarmed; heaved with them. You rubbed against them as you walked, you couldn't help yourself. Rub, rub, as you walked, wherever you went, there was no escape. Rub, rub, rub . . . You were never alone, always rubbing, touching, hearing, smelling it was delicious. Where are they now? Where are they now, all my friends . . . ?

[*The dog growls.*]

Growl, then. Bare your teeth. Eat me up, then. You've wanted to for long enough. Well, here's your chance. Go on, eat me. Eat me! Eat me!

[*The dog patters to the entrance. Her eyes follow it.*]

Where are you going? Nemmy, don't leave me alone . . . !

[*There is silence; the* WOMAN *is motionless. The* TWO MEN *appear, walking slowly towards the house. The woman stands up, hearing them.*]

Who is it? Oh, it's you . . .

[*The* 2ND MAN *comes in, followed by the* 1ST.]

2ND [*with a great effort.*]: Well, well . . . I'm back. Again . . .

[*Spent, he stands, immobilised.*]

WOMAN: And a friend. How nice.
1ST: Charming, charming.
WOMAN: Visitors are always welcome.
1ST: You are too kind.
WOMAN: Not at all.
1ST: Yes, yes . . .
WOMAN: How nice.

[*They sit down.*]

Did you have a good day, dear?

[*The* 2ND MAN *stands without movement, eyes shut.*]

Did you have a good day, dear?

[*There is no answer.*]

Did you have a good day, dear?
2ND [*opening his eyes*]: I had a day.
WOMAN: Yes, I know, but did you have a *good* day, dear?

[*No answer.*]

Did you have a good *day*, dear?
2ND: How do I know whether I had a good day?
WOMAN: But you must have had a good day or not a good day . . .

[*There is no answer.*]

Did you *have* a good *day*, dear?
2ND: Must we keep on about it? I had a *day*. Another *day*. Like
the last. And the one before that. It's over. Good, bad or
indifferent. Finished. Gone. That's all I ask. Now enough about
the day.

[*He recloses his eyes. The* WOMAN *turns to the* 1ST MAN.]

WOMAN: Did you have a good day?
1ST: Well, you know, life goes on. It comes to the same.
WOMAN: I see . . .
1ST: The object came as a surprise, of course.
WOMAN: Object?
1ST: A round, bent, straight object.
WOMAN: Really?
1ST: Metal. Half-buried.
WOMAN: Oh?
1ST: Useful in its time, I daresay . . .

[*There is a pause.*]

Though for what, I don't know . . .

[*There is a pause.*]

It seemed in good condition. But of course if the thing to which it was attached is no longer in existence, it's usefulness in that respect . . . diminishes . . .

[*There is a pause.*]

However, one must be optimistic. I was picking my way over the rocks this morning, as usual, when a thought struck me. Here I am, I thought, picking my way over the rocks this morning, as usual, and if I didn't know that yesterday was yesterday, today could be yesterday . . . Why not? What's to prove otherwise? And yet—here I am. Picking my way over the rocks. Yesterday's over and done with, though it was just like today. Today isn't yesterday yet, of course, but it will be. Tomorrow. Over and done with. Tomorrow too. In its time. One has only to wait. Tomorrow too. Over and done with. It comes to the same. Life goes on . . .

[*There is a pause.*]

Do you understand? Life goes on. With us or without us. It comes to the same. One must be optimistic . . .

2ND [*opening his eyes*]: Where is my bone?

[*There is a pause.*]

WOMAN: Your bone, dear? . . .

[*A silence.*]

There is no bone, dear . . .

[*The* 2ND MAN *looks at his wife. There is a silence.*]

WOMAN: There *was* a bone, dear. *Was*. But this is *is*. There is no bone, dear.

[*His face is crumbling rather frighteningly.*]

There *was* a bone . . .

1ST: It comes to the same. To have had or to have not had. If you had a bone today, tomorrow you could only say: there *was* a bone. Well, now, you can say it today. It comes to the same. There was a bone . . .

[*He and the* WOMAN *look anxiously at the* 2ND MAN *who, at last, moves his body and begins to sit down. This accomplished, he is motionless for a moment.*]

Life goes one. . .

[*The* 2ND MAN *begins to shake. His laughter is terrible. He is racked by it.*]

Bones are but bones, come what may . . . Come, come, let us look on the bright side.

[*The* 2ND MAN *stops shaking and looks up.*]

All is not lost.
We still have our health and strength.

2ND: You are quite right, my dear fellow. Bones are but bones. All is not lost. It comes to the same. Nothing is essential. Not bones, not bread, not even the satisfaction of knowing that one thinks that one's feet ache. Nothing. Look at me. All day I struggled from one foot to another, breathing in and breathing out, pushing the blood through my veins for what? For the *thought* that my wife had a bone for me. Not for the bone, for the thought of it. Who would have guessed I'd have got through today from one end to the other? But I've managed it again. And *no bone*. Still I breathe.

1ST: As I say . . .

WOMAN: Perhaps there'll be a bone tomorrow.

2ND: You miss the point!! Bones are irrelevant. I can live without them . . .

[*There is a pause.*]

Life grows simpler. One day I shall decide to give up this luxury of pushing air in and out of myself. A day or two later I shall say to myself: What? Still here? Still? Not even that? *What*, then? What? Is nothing essential . . . ?

1ST: Bones are one thing; breathing is another . . .

2ND: So you say . . .

[*There is a silence. The three sit, ruminating. The* TRAVELLER *and the* GIRL *appear. They stand at the entrance, looking at the three figures sitting motionless, a pathetic statuesque group. After a while the* WOMAN *looks up, turns her head and sees the* TRAVELLER.]

TRAVELLER: Don't be afraid, I'm your son.

[*She makes no response, but sits looking at him. The* 1ST MAN *jumps to his feet.*]

1ST: Didn't I tell you! I told you! The prisoners. They're back [*with tears in his eyes*]. Didn't I tell you? . . . [*to the* WOMAN] Well? Well?

[*She gets up and faces the* TRAVELLER.]

WOMAN: My . . . son?

TRAVELLER: Don't you remember? Don't you remember that boy you sent out with a light in his eyes? And a song on his lips? And a hope in his heart? Don't you remember?

WOMAN: I don't know . . . I'm not sure . . . Wait . . . Yes, wait . . . I think . . .

2ND: We have no son.

[*They look at him. He remains seated.*]

1ST: My dear chap . . .

2ND: We have no son. Get out and leave us alone.

[*The* WOMAN *turns to him.*]

WOMAN: What are you saying . . . ? Would you take this from me too? You pretend things have always been like this, but I know better. I have memories. Not many, but some, odd scraps. It wasn't always like this . . . Trees, do you deny there were trees? The world was full of things, full. I only have to remember them . . . Wait. Already, you see, already I remember something else. The sounds of the trees—Not leaves, something besides leaves. Birds. *Birds.*

2ND: No.

1ST: Birds?

WOMAN: Do you deny there were birds? [*To the* TRAVELLER.] Give me time, just give me time. I'll remember everything.

2ND: There were no birds!

WOMAN: I remember . . .

2ND: We've lived long enough without birds. Why complicate things? There are no birds, there are no trees, we have no son, still we live. *Still. What do you want?* To get them back, to lose them again? We live, that's enough. Let that be an end of it.

TRAVELLER: It's not enough.

2ND: We live.

TRAVELLER: It isn't enough just to *live.*

2ND: Enough for me.

TRAVELLER: This?

2ND: I live. Do I not? . . . Can you do more?

TRAVELLER: Yes.

2ND: Then go and do it somewhere else.

1ST: My dear chap, what are you saying?

2ND: I'm saying I am not interested.

1ST: But—*progress.* My dear chap, *progress* . . . He's here to help us . . .

[*The* 2ND MAN *puts his hands over his face and begins to shake.*]

TRAVELLER: What's the matter with him?

1ST: Laughing . . . He'll stop.

2ND: Help me to do what? Breathe? Look. See. I'm breathing already. He's too late. Stand up on my legs? But I'm on my legs. Look, here I am. [*Getting up*] What, then. What more? To breathe twice as fast? To stand on only *one* leg? Will you teach me to fly?

[*He shakes.*]

What then? What? What? What?

[*The* TRAVELLER *says nothing.*]

WOMAN: There were other things, all sorts of things . . .

2ND: There were other things. And we lived. Now there's nothing. And we live . . . I am not going through all that again!! Get out! Leave us alone. We don't want you! don't you understand?

[*There is a pause.*]

Yes, I remember. I remember everything. And I am not going through all that again!!

[*He turns to the* TRAVELLER.]

I'll tell you my ambition.

[*He shakes a moment.*]

I'll tell you my ambition. To stand, here, where I am, with my eyes closed, until I wish to sit down, and then to sit, there, with my eyes closed, until I wish to lie down, and then to lie, there, and sleep until I can say: Here I am at the beginning of another day; only a few hours, only a few hours and I shall be at the end of this day too, somehow, I don't know how, somehow . . . That's all I ask. Take your complications elsewhere. Try next door. Teach someone else to fly! Not me!! Not me!!

[*A pause.*]

Leave us alone for the love of . . . !

1ST: He doesn't mean it. He's, he's . . .

[*The* TRAVELLER *turns to go.*]

You're not going! Listen. I agree. I agree with you. I'll help. I'll come with you . . . Tomorrow . . .

TRAVELLER [*quietly*]: You stupid bastards. Do you think you have any choice?

[*The* TRAVELLER *looks at him, and goes out, leaving them standing, statuesque. The* GIRL *is waiting; the* TRAVELLER *comes up to her.*]

GIRL: Are we going? Can we go now?

TRAVELLER: We'd better find somewhere to sleep. Tomorrow we'll start.

GIRL: Start what?

TRAVELLER: Building. Again. Come on.

[*They begin to walk off. There is a growl, and a pattering of feet. The* GIRL *screams, terrified, as the dog rushes at the man. There is a scuffle. The* TRAVELLER *raises his clenched fists again and again, bringing them down with all his force. The* WOMAN *gives a kind of scream from the house. There is silence, except for the* TRAVELLER'S *panting as he looks down at the dog.*]

[*The* WOMAN *stands at the entrance, staring out into the night.*]

WOMAN: Nemmy . . . Nemmy . . . They've killed him. They've killed my dog . . . They've killed my dog . . .

[*He walks off with the* GIRL.]

[*The* TRAVELLER *and the* GIRL. *The* TRAVELLER *is looking across the city.*]

GIRL: I'm tired.

TRAVELLER: Just a moment. Just give me a moment . . .

GIRL: They don't want you, do they? Then why stay here? I don't need anyone else. I've put myself in your hands. You can do

whatever you like with me. You can kill me, when you feel
like it . . . Isn't that enough for you? Isn't it possible for people
to live on their own?

TRAVELLER: No . . .

GIRL: Are you crying again?

TRAVELLER: No.

GIRL: Then what's the matter?

TRAVELLER: I'd forgotten what it would be like.

GIRL: What?

TRAVELLER: Do you know how long it'll take to build this city?
And it may happen again. And again. And again . . .

[*Pause.*]

GIRL: How long have there been people?

TRAVELLER: Not long . . .

GIRL: I'm tired.

TRAVELLER: I'm coming.

[*He turns to her; she puts her arms round his waist, and they begin
to walk off. He stops, and looks round.*]

We can use these stones.

GIRL: Tomorrow.

[*Together they walk off.*]

A SLIGHT ACCIDENT

First performance at the Nottingham Playhouse, October 1961

PENELOPE   Joan Heal

CAMILLA   Rosamund Greenwood

RODGER   Patrick Blackwell

Directed by FRANK DUNLOP

CHARACTERS
in order of appearance

PENELOPE

HARRY

CAMILLA

ACTRESS 1

ACTRESS 2

ACTOR 1

ACTOR 2

RODGER

A SLIGHT ACCIDENT

[*There is the sound of a shot.*]

[*As the curtain rises* PENELOPE *is standing, becomingly, with an equivocal expression on her face and a revolver, still smoking, in her hand. At some distance lies the body of a man.* PENELOPE, *looking perhaps rather as might a woman of means who had just broken her husband's favourite piece of antique china, looks at the body, without moving towards it, then at the revolver. It continues to smoke. She waves it about, blows down the barrel, coughs, fans away gracefully the trace of gun-smoke still hanging in the air, and considers the situation.*]

PENELOPE: Oh dear . . .

[*She goes up to the body, peers at it without stooping.*]

Harry . . . Harry dear, don't be ridiculous . . . really, if you can't take a joke . . . Will you please get up . . . Harry, do get up . . . Harry! Harry?

[*She gently nudges it with her toe.*]

Harry?

[*No answer. She goes to the telephone, dials, and waits.*]

Hallo, Camilla darling, Am I disturbing you? . . . You are? Oh . . . I wondered if you could come up for a few minutes . . . No, I *can't* wait. I've just done something rather tiresome and I need company. Come and watch the rest of the— My husband isn't much company at the moment . . . You don't know at *all* what I mean . . . Darling, *please* . . . Yes, we've had it fixed . . . Yes, the picture's perfect now . . . That's sweet of you.

[*She hangs up, switches on the television, looks at the body again.*]

Everything happens to me . . .

[*She takes another look at the body, goes to the door, turns back as though coming in for the first time.*]

Penelope darling—Oh ...

[*She hurriedly covers the body with a bearskin rug. She arranges meticulously and with taste several cushions on the rug. The doorbell rings. She goes to answer it. The television comes on as she comes back with* CAMILLA.]

CAMILLA: Penelope darling, what *has* happened?

[PENELOPE *says nothing. Her eyes on* PENELOPE, CAMILLA *sits before the television, and is drawn into it.* PENELOPE *walks to and fro, rehearsing her lines.*]

ACTRESS 1: I've had this to say for twenty years: you're rotten, you've always been rotten and you always will be rotten.
ACTRESS 2: You despise me ...
ACTRESS 1: You killed my brother. You drove my son to suicide. You ruined my cousin. All you touch you defile.

[*Sobs.*]

ACTRESS 1: You sent my husband mad; you corrupted his nephew.
ACTRESS 2: Why do you hate me?

[*Sobs. Sound of door opening.*]

ACTRESS 1: You're filthy. Filthy.
ACTRESS 2: Philip! Thank God you're safe.

[*Sound of door closing.*]

ACTOR 1: My God I need a drink.

[*Sound of door opening.*]

ACTRESS 1: I'm going to my room.

[*Sound of door closing.*]

ACTRESS 2: Philip, where's . . . ?
ACTOR 1: Dead.

[*Sound of breath being caught.*]

ACTRESS 2: How . . . ?
ACTOR 1: Tincture of iodine. Evelyn, can't we start afresh? Go away somewhere?
ACTRESS 2: Where?
ACTOR 1: Anywhere. Trucial Oman.
ACTRESS 2: You mean—Together? You're vile. Vile . . .
ACTOR 1: You fool. Don't you realise this is your last chance?
ACTRESS 2: I can't take any more, I can't, I can't!!!

[*Sobs. Sound of door opening.*]

ACTRESS 1: I heard a shot.
ACTOR 1: What!
ACTRESS 2: Not . . .

[*Sound of door opening. Sound of doorbell.*]

Oh God . . . Vincent!

[*Sound of door closing.*]

ACTOR 2: Quite a pretty picture, isn't it? Well, the time has come.
ACTOR 1: My God I need a drink.

[*Sound of telephone.*]

ACTRESS 1: Don't answer it! It's a trap!

[*Sound of door closing. Sound of doorbell.*]

ACTRESS 2: Look out, he's got a knife!
ACTOR 2: You've had your last drink, you swine!

[*Sound of a shot. Sound of breath being caught. Sound of gurgling. Silence. Sound of a glassful of whisky and soda dripping onto a tiled fireplace. Silence. Sound of a body dropping onto the floor.*]

ACTRESS 2: He's ...
ACTOR 1: Dead.
ACTRESS 2: You'd better go.
ACTRESS 1: And leave you ... ?
ACTRESS 2: Yes. Leave me. Go.

[*Sound of door closing.*]

ACTOR 1: Coming, Claire?

[*Sound of door opening.*]

ACTOR 2: You'll be all right?

[*Sound of door closing.*]

ACTRESS 2: I'll be all right. Leave the gun.

[*Sound of door closing. Silence. A shot. Silence. Sound of a body falling on to the floor. Music.* CAMILLA *looks round at* PENELOPE, *arguing with herself. She switches off.*]

CAMILLA: I'll not watch part two after all.
PENELOPE: No?
CAMILLA: I don't think so. All the interesting characters are dead already.
PENELOPE: That's what I always say.
CAMILLA: Where's Harry?
PENELOPE: Who?
CAMILLA: Your husband ...
PENELOPE: What about him?
CAMILLA: Where is he?
PENELOPE: Why?
CAMILLA: I'm only asking.
PENELOPE: Why do you ask, what do you mean, do you think I've murdered him or something, why are you looking at me like that? As a matter of fact he's lying down.
CAMILLA: Isn't he well?

PENELOPE: No. Yes. I don't know.

CAMILLA: You *must* know.

PENELOPE: Why must I?

CAMILLA: But darling—

PENELOPE: I don't live in my husband's pocket. Harry's a free agent; if he wants to be well or unwell he doesn't have to give me an account of it. Do you think I go running around after Harry saying, are you well, Harry, are you still well?

CAMILLA: Forget I asked...

PENELOPE: He wanted to lie down, so he lay down.

CAMILLA: All *right*, darling.

[*Pause.*]

So what's the trouble?

[PENELOPE *looks at her.*]

You said you'd done something stupid.

PENELOPE: I didn't say that at all. I don't know what you mean.

CAMILLA: Penelope darling, you rang me up—

PENELOPE: I didn't say stupid.

CAMILLA: Let's not play with words...

PENELOPE: Why not, words are important. What do we have to play with but words? I'm not going to have you coming down here at a moment's notice accusing me of being stupid.

CAMILLA: Oh, dear...

PENELOPE: What I said was 'tiresome'. It was an accident.

CAMILLA: What was?

PENELOPE: To be stupid you have to do it on purpose. It's like breaking the handle off a cup; if you do it on purpose that's stupid but if it's an accident it's tiresome, that's all, certainly not stupid. I didn't do it on purpose... I don't think...

CAMILLA: You didn't.

PENELOPE: Why should I?

CAMILLA: But why all this fuss about breaking a handle off a cup?

PENELOPE: I haven't broken any handles, darling, it's nothing to do with handles.

CAMILLA: I see.

PENELOPE: You don't see.

CAMILLA: Very true.

[*Pause.*]

Are you going to give me a drink?

[PENELOPE *begins to go through the usual motions.*]

I do like your curtains . . . Of course, you don't *have* to tell me anything . . .

PENELOPE: Give me time, darling . . . Some things are so silly they're embarrassing. I mean, there's the normal course of events carrying itself along as usual, in a nice straight grey line, and then suddenly out of the blue there's this ludicrous occurrence, spoiling the whole natural sequence.

[*She is still busying herself with the drinks.*]

I mean, life is full of actions you couldn't possibly explain. Nearly everything we do is—inexplicable. And what difference does it make if the result of a particular action happens to be rather—extreme? . . .

[*She turns.*]

Camilla darling . . .

CAMILLA: Penelope . . . What's that?

PENELOPE: What?

CAMILLA: That heap.

PENELOPE: Heap?

CAMILLA: There.

PENELOPE: I don't see anything.

CAMILLA: It looks like a body covered with a bearskin rug, with cushions for camouflage.

PENELOPE: Ridiculous.

CAMILLA: May I look?

PENELOPE: It's a bearskin rug, there's nothing there, I don't know what you're talking about—I forbid you to touch it! I asked you up because I thought I could rely upon you as a friend.

CAMILLA: I'd like to help—

PENELOPE: I took you for a woman of delicacy and understanding?

CAMILLA: But I don't know what to be understanding *about*.

PENELOPE: And all you can do is pry into my life and peer under my carpets as though you expect to find bodies under them all, and then you accuse me of shooting my husband.

CAMILLA: Shooting your—?

PENELOPE: There you go again!

CAMILLA: But I didn't mention—

PENELOPE: Then why make these grotesque allusions to a perfectly ordinary rug and a few cushions?

CAMILLA: It was a joke, darling—

PENELOPE: A joke! You think it's a joke!

CAMILLA: As for your husband, I didn't mention your husband. It just looked like an anonymous body, that's all; it could be anyone's husband.

PENELOPE: And I suppose you're thinking: ah, I didn't notice the shot because there were shots in the play and I mistook the sound of Penelope shooting her husband for someone in the play getting shot. And now you're trying to think back to whether there was one more shot than there were bodies. You've got it all worked out, haven't you? I daresay you've decided on a motive too. Well, let me inform you that in all the years of our marriage Harry and I have never once quarrelled, not once. Show me another couple you can say that about, give me their names. Harry and I have lived in perfect harmony. *There*, there are the slippers I laid out ready for him, just where he knows he can find them; there is the bunch of flowers he brings me home regularly every single

Thursday, for some reason. My God, I do think one could expect at least one's friends to show a little understanding and sympathy and not go leaping to the most bizzare conclusions at every opportunity. Well, it's as they say: you climb in company, but you fall alone, and woe betide you if you expect your closest friend to stretch out a hand to check your descent.

CAMILLA: You're not unique, you know.

PENELOPE: Hm?

CAMILLA: I've never quarrelled with Rodger either. Rodger's never quarrelled in his life; he doesn't believe in it. Rodger thinks one should never raise one's voice after the age of two.

PENELOPE: Then you know what I'm talking about.

CAMILLA: I know what you're talking about, darling.

PENELOPE: Another drink?

CAMILLA: Yes please . . . May one ask one question?

PENELOPE: Hm?

CAMILLA: You won't think I'm prying?

PENELOPE: Probably.

CAMILLA: That is a boot, is it?

PENELOPE: Not at all. It's a shoe.

CAMILLA: I see.

[PENELOPE *hands her a drink.*]

PENELOPE: It's been one of those days, you know?

[*Pause.*]

CAMILLA: The evenings are drawing in . . .

PENELOPE: Darling, you don't have to fill in the pauses.

[*Pause.*]

PENELOPE: Language is so limited.

CAMILLA: Hm?

PENELOPE: Who was that scientist who was once caught, alone in his room, dropping a little bit of cotton wool into a basin, to see whether he could hear it hit the bottom?

[CAMILLA *takes a long look at her.*]

Can you imagine him trying to explain himself? Of *course* he knew he wouldn't be able to hear it. He just did it—because he knew it wouldn't work . . . Let me start at the beginning, darling. You see, what happened—

[*Door bell. Pause.*]

CAMILLA: Shall I go?

[PENELOPE *nods.* CAMILLA *goes; she comes back with* RODGER, *who is dressed as one might expect a stockbroker's son to be dressed at ten in the evening.*]

RODGER: I'm *not* following you about, dear; it's just that I'd made the cocoa—
CAMILLA: I'm sorry, darling, Rodger's come up.
RODGER: You don't have to apologise. How are you, Penelope?
PENELOPE: Oh, I'm—first class.
RODGER: Jolly good. And Harry?
PENELOPE: He's first class.
RODGER: Mhm. Well, dear, what are we going to do about the cocoa?
CAMILLA: Do we have to do anything about it?
RODGER: It's down there getting cold. [*To Penelope*] I go into the kitchen as I do every evening, make the cocoa, take it into the lounge and I find my wife's disappeared. Upset the routine completely.
CAMILLA: Go and drink the cocoa if you want to.
RODGER: It isn't the cocoa, dear, it's the principle of the thing. Whether I drink the cocoa or not, the routine's been upset; you can't get away from it. I say, what's that?
PENELOPE: Nothing.

RODGER: Yes, but what is it?

PENELOPE: Why is everyone so inquisitive? I invite people up and all they do is poke around asking what's this, what's that? It's an Axminster carpet wrapped up in a bearskin rug.

RODGER: But—

PENELOPE: The cleaners are calling for it in the morning—the carpet, the rug and the cushions. They all need cleaning.

RODGER: Yes, but—

PENELOPE: Down the centre of the carpet is a long pole to make it easier to carry the carpet and on the end of the pole is a shoe, so that the person carrying the carpet will not be injured by the end of the pole. The shoe is a safety measure. Now I hope everyone's satisfied.

RODGER: There seem to be two shoes.

PENELOPE: Then there must be two poles, mustn't there? What will you drink?

RODGER: Cocoa. Where's Harry?

PENELOPE: Whisky or gin?

RODGER: Yes, please. Where's—?

PENELOPE [pouring a drink]: He's out of town.

RODGER: Out of town?

PENELOPE: Yes.

RODGER: I thought he was in town.

PENELOPE: He was in town, now he's out of town.

CAMILLA: Not lying down.

RODGER: Out of town not lying down?

PENELOPE: He's out of town lying down. Is there anything to prevent that?

CAMILLA: If he's out of town how do you know he's lying down?

PENELOPE: He rang me up.

CAMILLA: To say he was lying down.

PENELOPE: Yes. He rang me up to say he was out of town, and that he was lying down. He was lying down when he rang me up. Do you mind?

CAMILLA: Lying down in a telephone box.

PENELOPE: No, darling, in a hotel bedroom. He rang me from an out-of-town bedside telephone to say he was lying down.

[*Pause.*]

RODGER: Is Harry in the habit of—?

PENELOPE: Why are you persecuting me?

CAMILLA: It just seems a little unusual . . .

PENELOPE: What are you insinuating? That he isn't out of town lying down? That he's in town standing up? Is that what you're getting at?

CAMILLA: No, darling . . .

PENELOPE: Do you think I have him standing up in a cupboard somewhere? Do you? Do you want to search my cupboards? Really, this is too bad.

[*Pause.*]

RODGER: Leeds?

CAMILLA: What?

RODGER: I was talking to Penelope.

PENELOPE: What?

RODGER: Leeds?

PENELOPE: Leads what?

RODGER: The town Leeds.

PENELOPE: The town leads what?

RODGER: Is it the town Leeds?

PENELOPE: Is what the town Leeds?

RODGER: Is Harry in the town Leeds?

PENELOPE: No.

RODGER: He was last year.

PENELOPE: Well he isn't this year.

[*Pause.*]

CAMILLA: Where then?

PENELOPE: Oh . . . Hull.

[*Pause.*]

CAMILLA: Why go to Hull to lie down?
PENELOPE: I don't want to pursue this subject.
CAMILLA: All right, darling.

[*Pause.*]

RODGER: Why not?
PENELOPE: I just don't.
RODGER: Mhm.
PENELOPE: He had to go to Hull to see a client.
CAMILLA: In a hotel.
PENELOPE: In an office, in an office.
RODGER: Then they went to the hotel—
PENELOPE: Then *he* went to the hotel, since he felt unwell, and lay on the bed and rang me up. Do you want his telephone number as well!
RODGER: I could give him a ring—
PENELOPE: Well you're not going to. I'm not going to have him pestered by all and sundry when he's not well . . . Poor Harry . . .
RODGER: Poor old Harry . . . It's his own fault, of course.
PENELOPE: What do you mean?
RODGER: Breaking his routine. It leads to trouble. He goes to Hull, a thing he never does; he becomes ill. Naturally. He should have let the client come to London. Let the client be sick.
CAMILLA: What are you talking about?
RODGER: Look at me. Am I ever ill. No. Why?
CAMILLA: Because you haven't the imagination.
RODGER: Because I stick to routine. Because I have every action catalogued, right down to the blowing of my nose at set intervals.
PENELOPE: Catalogued?

RODGER: I keep a book. A sort of manual of running instructions. I've worked it out over the years. What's childhood for if not to learn one's running routine? By the time I was twenty I knew precisely what I'd be doing any minute of the day. It's the only way to live safely. Behind the facade, no, the bastion of habit, of routine, anarchy lurks, waiting to spring...

CAMILLA: Rodger dear—

RODGER: Look at this case in the paper today. A hairdresser's assistant in Balham is working quietly along a row of seven ladies sitting under the hairdriers when suddenly he takes up a pair of scissors and stabs all seven of them one after another. Why did it happen? I'll tell you: he lost respect for routine, he threw his habits over-board. He left the well-ordered terrain of habituality and struck off into the jungle of infinite possibility, where every step is into unknown country. Think of him. I may continue to dry the hair of these women who mean nothing to me, he says to himself. I may go along the line asking are they comfortable and offering them the *Tatler* and *Country Life*; but equally I may not. But if not, what? Indeed, what not?

[*Pause.*]

CAMILLA: What are you trying to prove?

RODGER: That I'm invulnerable; impregnable; safe.

CAMILLA: That you'll never stab a woman with a pair of scissors while she's sitting under a hairdrier.

RODGER: Yes, for instance. Tell me, have I ever committed a crime? Ever run anyone over or been run over? Ever missed a train? I'm a creature of habit; I'm as safe as houses.

PENELOPE: You shouldn't be too sure.

RODGER: Well, here's the proof.

PENELOPE: Where?

RODGER: Here. Me. I sit here after thirty-nine years without a scar, without a worry, without a stain on my character; I did today what I did yesterday, and I shall do tomorrow what I did today. Nothing went wrong today, nothing can go wrong tomorrow. If I meet the untoward on my way, I shall size it up from a distance, and walk gingerly round it.

CAMILLA: What have you got there, Rodger?

[*Rodger, in making himself more comfortable in his chair, has removed the hard lump from under his cushion. He stares at it.*]

PENELOPE: Be careful, Rodger, it may have a hair-trigger.

RODGER: It's not loaded, obviously.

PENELOPE: D'you want to try it?

[*Rodger examines it.*]

CAMILLA: Loaded?

[*He nods.*]

PENELOPE: You see?

RODGER: Isn't it rather dangerous, leaving loaded revolvers lying around?

PENELOPE: It isn't leaving them lying around that's dangerous, it's picking them up and pulling the trigger. There you are, you see, the man of habit, sitting drinking gin and tonic with a loaded revolver pointed at your wife.

RODGER: The safety catch is on; I do know a little about revolvers.

PENELOPE: Do you know how little one finger has to move in order to pull the trigger?

RODGER: I tell you the safety catch is on.

PENELOPE: Do you know how little the thumb has to move to put it off?

[*Rodger smells the barrel.*]

RODGER: It's been fired.

PENELOPE: Has it?

RODGER: One shot.

PENELOPE: Really?

RODGER: Recently.

[*Pause.*]

PENELOPE: Yes. That's right. It was me.

RODGER: You?

PENELOPE: Yes. I pulled the trigger.

CAMILLA: When?

PENELOPE: This evening. I had it in my hand and the trigger got pulled.

RODGER: By you.

PENELOPE: Who else?

CAMILLA: So there *was* an extra shot.

RODGER: During the play. Of course. There was a shot, and no one fell down. It seemed rather strange at the time.

PENELOPE: That's what it was, you see.

CAMILLA: What were you firing at? Or was it an accident?

PENELOPE: More drinks, anyone?

RODGER: Of course it was an accident, what else could it have been?

PENELOPE: More drinks?

CAMILLA: Was it?

PENELOPE: What?

CAMILLA: An accident?

PENELOPE: Now let's see, yours was a gin as well, wasn't it? . . . Yes, of course it was an accident.

CAMILLA: You just picked it up and it went off.

PENELOPE: I just picked it up and—pulled the trigger.

RODGER: By accident.

PENELOPE: Naturally . . . That is to say . . .

CAMILLA: What?

PENELOPE: That is to say, I pulled the *trigger* on purpose. If that's what you mean.

CAMILLA: What else could we mean, darling?

RODGER: So it *wasn't* an accident.

PENELOPE: It *was*.

CAMILLA: But you did it deliberately.

PENELOPE: I didn't do it deliberately . . . I did it on purpose . . .

CAMILLA: *Darling* . . .

PENELOPE: Oh, *really* . . . Why are you so *obtuse*? Why do you pretend everything's so *simple*?

CAMILLA: There's accident, darling, and there's design, darling—

PENELOPE: And there's Rodger sitting there with a glass in his hand, about to raise it to his lips.

RODGER: I don't get the drift.

PENELOPE: Did you pick it up deliberately?

RODGER: Yes . . . Well—half deliberately . . .

PENELOPE: *Half* deliberately; *Rodger* . . . You picked it up, on purpose to drink it, without deliberation . . . You raise it to your lips, and take a sip, on purpose to drink it, without deliberation. And if the glass contained poison, and by some accident nothing happened to stop you—

RODGER: But it doesn't.

PENELOPE: Or if it were not a glass of gin and tonic but a revolver, and you didn't raise it to your lips without deliberation but raised it with your finger on the trigger, without deliberation, and somebody said 'Pull it' and you pulled . . .

RODGER: I don't know what you're talking about.

PENELOPE: I picked up the revolver, just as you picked up that glass; I put my finger on the trigger, as one does automatically; I held it up like this, as one does; and . . .

RODGER: You *pulled* the *trigger*.

PENELOPE: —And by some—accident, by some mischance . . . nothing happened to stop me . . .

[*Slight pause.*]

PENELOPE: Of all the thousand and one things that could have happened, nothing did . . . Suppose, for instance, there'd been a mouse.

RODGER: A mouse?

PENELOPE: A *mouse*, yes . . .

RODGER: You shot at a mouse?

PENELOPE: No, Rodger, I didn't shoot at a mouse, but let's say there *was* a mouse; which ran out from under that chair.

RODGER: Impossible.

PENELOPE: What's impossible about it?

RODGER: There are no mice.

PENELOPE: How do you know? How do you know what's behind the wainscot?

RODGER: If there were mice in this flat, there'd be mice in our flat.

PENELOPE: We could have our own private mice, couldn't we?

RODGER: No, because they'd have to pass our flat to get here.

PENELOPE: Well they did. They came during the day, while you were out. Or watching television. There were mice on television and you thought you were hearing television mice scuttling by, just as with the shot. My finger was on the trigger, when suddenly—out from under that chair, frightened by a cat, ran the mouse.

RODGER: Cat! What cat?

PENELOPE: A cat, any cat. A cat from downstairs. It came up, attracted by the smell of milk.

RODGER: There's no cat downstairs. We have no cat; the Fergusons on the first floor, they have no cat; the Hartleys on the ground floor, they have no cat. Even the porter has no cat. Then whose cat was it?

PENELOPE: It was *no one's* cat. It was a stray cat. The town's full of stray cats, wild cats, cats that have never known a proper home. Born in coal cellars and, and bicycle sheds, fending for themselves. It's the old story. They eat what they can; it's a hard life. This one was looking for mice on the stairs.

CAMILLA: You said it smelt milk.

PENELOPE: It smelt milk and forgot the mice. But when it got up here it smelt mice and forgot the milk. The cat crept behind the chair and the mouse, which had been attracted by the smell of the biscuits I was to have with my milk—

CAMILLA: You don't drink milk, Penelope . . .

PENELOPE: Camilla, *please* . . . The mouse, alarmed, bounded from under the chair—

RODGER: Followed by the cat.

PENELOPE: Followed by the cat, and I, surprised, forgot that I'd been about to accidentally, on purpose, without deliberation, pull the trigger, and . . . didn't. That would have been an accident, wouldn't it? So, by the same token, it was an accident that, as you say, we have no mice; no cats. And that's how the unfortunate accident happened. . .

CAMILLA: What accident?

PENELOPE: Darlings, I'm forgetting your glasses.

CAMILLA: What accident?

[PENELOPE *turns to her; they look at each other for some time.*]

Penelope . . .

PENELOPE: *Life*—is by no means as straightforward as it's supposed to be.

RODGER: If it wasn't a mouse, what *were* you aiming at?

PENELOPE: You think we live in the age of reason, don't you? You think we can put our life under the microscope, prod it this way and that way with a little pair of tweezers and say: ah, yes; I did this because of this and this because of this. How simple!

RODGER: Penelope, what—?

PENELOPE: Ten years ago, on my way to visit a taxidermist, I got stuck in a lift between the fourth and fifth floors.

[RODGER *scratches his head.*]

Three-quarters of an hour later, coming down, between the fourth floor and the third floor, I got stuck in the same lift, together with the same stranger I was stuck in the lift with on the way up. Improbable? *Yes.* But it happened. That's what caused it ...

RODGER: Caused what?

PENELOPE: That's how I met Harry. And off went the chain of events on its immutable course. And what d'you think I had to do with it?

RODGER: I don't get the drift ...

PENELOPE: I mean we *pretend*, Rodger, we *pretend* ... that we're in control, that we decide ... Well maybe we *do*; but what *makes* us decide ...?

RODGER: I don't agree with anything you're saying—

PENELOPE: Of course you don't; you're not able to. You think we play our lives like fish.

RODGER: Yes, like fish—

PENELOPE: You think we stand on the banks of the river of life, all dressed up in our oilskins of habit, catching events like salmon as they leap past. It may seem so to you, Rodger; but are the events, in reality, catching us?

RODGER: What *were* you aiming at?

[*Pause.*]

PENELOPE: Who, me ... ?

[*Slight pause.*]

RODGER: Of course we're in control; we can choose, can't we?

PENELOPE: D'you think I had a *choice* of marrying Harry or not marrying Harry?

RODGER: I'm not talking about Harry. I'm talking about life—

PENELOPE: I'm talking about Harry. I had no choice.

RODGER: Nonsense ...

PENELOPE: Of course I had no choice. We met, perforce, in a lift. And there we were later, drinking good coffee after a delicious meal in an expensive restaurant ... It was a foregone conclusion; so much so that he didn't even bother to ask me; he *told* me. We'll get married, he said. Yes, I said. Naturally; of course; what else? Why not? . . . A dreadful gypsy violinist scraped his bow plaintively two tables away, while I sipped chartreuse; of course, why not, what else, who could think otherwise . . . ?

RODGER: You could have said no.

PENELOPE: Of course I couldn't, how ridiculous.

RODGER: I don't see anthing ridiculous about it. Did he *force* you to say yes?

PENELOPE: He didn't have to *force* me. I had no *choice*.

RODGER: I don't understand.

PENELOPE: I couldn't do otherwise.

RODGER: I don't understand.

PENELOPE: I *wanted* to.

RODGER: You wanted to do otherwise?

PENELOPE: I *wanted* to *marry Harry*.

RODGER: Well there you are!

PENELOPE: There you are.

RODGER: And if you'd wanted to say no—

PENELOPE: But I didn't *want*—to say no . . . I wanted to say yes, I had no choice—but to want to say yes.

RODGER: Then why blame Harry?

PENELOPE: I'm not blaming Harry, why do you continually get the wrong end of the stick? I don't regret marrying him. Ours is not the kind of marriage one regrets. Far from it. Never once has Harry ever behaved in any way other than as I would have expected him to. Never once has he given me the slightest cause to feel he was dissatisfied or restless or wanted to see someone else's face at the breakfast table, just for once. Our life together has been one continuous stream of marital harmony . . .

CAMILLA: Tell Rodger what you were aiming at, darling.

PENELOPE: Aiming what at?

CAMILLA: The revolver.

PENELOPE: I wasn't aiming it. I just pointed it at something.

RODGER: At what?

PENELOPE: At a target.

RODGER: Are you in the habit of doing target practice in the evening?

PENELOPE: Habit has nothing to do with it. Besides, as I said, it was an accident.

CAMILLA: Because you have no mice.

PENELOPE: Yes, because I have no mice. And because plaster didn't fall from the ceiling and because the telephone didn't ring and because the world didn't suddenly come to an end; really, this is like an inquisition! One would think there were nothing else in the world but why I let off this silly gun! As though the whole Universe were centred in one accidental revolver shot! Really, you're both positively *medieval*.

RODGER: We don't have to stay if you don't want us to.

PENELOPE: I do want you to. I want to be able to talk to friends intimate enough to understand without passing judgement.

RODGER: What on?

PENELOPE: Me.

CAMILLA: Why should we?

PENELOPE: Why indeed? Why should anyone pass judgement on anyone in this strange, haphazard, accidental life?

[*Pause. A sob.* PENELOPE *is crying.* RODGER *flaps his arms.*]

CAMILLA: Penelope . . .

PENELOPE: Don't speak to me. I don't want to be spoken to. I want absolute silence . . . I know I'm being incredibly tiresome.

RODGER: Not at all—

PENELOPE: Don't contradict me. I am . . . I'm being incredibly tiresome and gauche . . . Dragging you away from your television, as though real life is more important . . . I was brought up in the old-fashioned way, you see; to think of friends as friends. But of course it's all a mockery. Life isn't to be taken seriously. It's just a cheap imitation of a television play. So undramatic . . . The most incredible things happen suddenly out of the blue, as though they've been stuck in by accident, and the last act doesn't resolve a thing. Life is an affront to the intelligence, I realise that; badly written, badly acted, and apparently not directed at all . . .

RODGER: I think you should take a sedative and go to bed.

PENELOPE: What solution does that produce to which problem?

[*Pause.*]

CAMILLA: And you hit it.

PENELOPE: Hit what?

CAMILLA: The target.

PENELOPE: What target?

CAMILLA: The one you were aiming at.

PENELOPE: I wasn't aiming at it, I just pointed the gun at it.

CAMILLA: But you did.

PENELOPE: Hit it?

CAMILLA: Yes.

PENELOPE: Yes.

CAMILLA: Hm.

[*Pause.*]

PENELOPE: The first things I ever noticed about Harry were his intelligence and his poise. He was never surprised. This is a logical world, he used to say; why be surprised if one thing happens rather than another? If a lift breaks down there's good reason for it. So while other men would have banged on the sides with their fists and walked up and down and pressed all the buttons, Harry simply divided his *Times* in two, and he sat on the foreign news in one corner while I sat on the home news in another, and for the next twenty minutes he explained to me Einstein's Special Theory of Relativity. Life, Harry used to say, is reason. Quarrelling, Harry used to say, is the last resort of the feeble-minded. Surprise, hope and despair, Harry used to say, are the three ugly sisters in the tale of Man's quest towards intellectual maturity . . .

CAMILLA: And down it fell . . .

PENELOPE: Mine has been the perfect marriage!

RODGER: Down what fell?

CAMILLA: The target.

PENELOPE: Yes, it fell down.

CAMILLA: Lay down.

RODGER: The target. Lay down?

PENELOPE: Yes, Rodger, the target lay down.

RODGER: I don't get the drift.

CAMILLA: No, dear; you don't get the drift.

PENELOPE: Because there isn't any drift to get.

[*Pause.*]

CAMILLA: You are so smug, Rodger.

RODGER: What?

CAMILLA: You're so *smug*.

RODGER: What are you talking about *now*?

CAMILLA: You think nothing can ever happen to you. You think nothing can ever go wrong.

RODGER: Of course it can't. I've explained. I'm impregnable.

CAMILLA: You're insufferable.

RODGER: I don't think you'd better have any more gin, dear . . .

CAMILLA: Very well . . . I have a lover.

RODGER: What the devil are you on about now?

CAMILLA: I have a *lover*.

RODGER: Nonsense; it's not your habit to—

CAMILLA: Not my habit! You don't know anything about my habits! What do you think I think of when you're away, during the day? It's been my habit for years. What are you smiling at? Haven't you noticed the gleam in my eye when you opened the door in the evening and said hallo, dear, and kissed me on the right cheek? Did you think my supressed yawns were boredom? No, they were satiation.

RODGER: I think you're going a bit far—

CAMILLA: How often have I longed for a loaded revolver as you sat smugly asking if I'd had a good day?

RODGER: *Really, Camilla ...*

CAMILLA: What do you know, Rodger? What—do—you—know?

[*Pause.* RODGER *picks up the revolver, goes over to* CAMILLA, *and puts it into her hand.*]

RODGER: Here you are. Hold it. Point it at me. I have the courage of my convictions. Pull back the safety catch. Pull the trigger.

[*She pulls the trigger. Pause.*]

CAMILLA: Oh dear ...

[*Pause.*]

I didn't have any lover ... Is that how ... ?

PENELOPE: Yes. That's how it happened to me.

THE PEDAGOGUE

A Monodrama

First performance at the Questors Theatre, Ealing, June 1963

Played by LAWRENCE IRVIN

Directed by JOHN MILES-BROWN

First professional production, Theatre-in-the-Round, Scarborough, Summer 1963

Played by DAVID JARRETT

Directed by STEPHEN JOSEPH

THE PEDAGOGUE

[*A classroom. A fair amount of noise, of chattering, laughing, desk-lids slamming, etc. When it is at its height the door opens, the noise diminishes somewhat, the door closes. The* SCHOOLMASTER *walks to his desk. Pause.*]

In the beginning—

[*Pause. The hubbub continues for a moment. Then the* SCHOOL-MASTER *gives a single hard rap with his cane on the desk. Silence. Slight pause.*]

Do you hear it?

[*Slight pause.*]

It's known as 'silence'. Prick your ears up; make sure you'll know it next time you meet it. In case you've forgotten the word, I'll write it out for you.

[*He does. Rather squeakily in block capitals on the blackboard.*]

It's what I'm accustomed to hear when I enter a classroom.

[*Slight pause. Somebody titters.*]

Somebody finds it funny?

[*Silence descends again.*]

Who has the blackboard rubber?

[*He rubs out.*]

Very well . . . Phipps, why is your exercise book on my desk? . . . What? . . . I did? Hm . . .

[*He leafs through the book, breathing hard.*]

'My favourite sport' . . .

[*Pause. He sighs. Pause. He shuts the book.*]

Very well, very well. [*Loudly.*] In the beginning was the Word.

[*Slight pause.*]

Brown, what was in the beginning? Quite right, very good, the Word. In the beginning . . . was . . .the Word . . . And the Word was Smith! Why are you staring at the ceiling? You'll find no instruction up there . . . Nor under your desk, Smith, don't scuttle under your desk whenever you're spoken to, Smith, *come out*, Green what are you sniggering at? Smith, I would refer you to one wiser than myself: 'Look not to the heavens for thy instruction, nor to the stars for they are beyond thee; and look not to the earth for thy instruction, not to the ant which labours nor to the firmament of thy bowels, for they are beneath thee', Green, I shall attend to you later. 'Look rather before thee, neither up nor down but before thee, for it is at thine own height that instruction lies.' Ahead, Smith; not up; not down . . . Better, yes, better . . . In the beginning— *what*, Smith? Was the . . . Not up, Smith, not down; was what? . . . Word, yes, word, right, very well, good . . . Word . . .

[*He writes it up. Pause. He rubs it out. He sighs.*]

Perkins, may one ask the reason for the expression of smugness? . . . Yes, Perkins, you. Perhaps you would care to stand up and explain to the class the reason why you consider this point in time an occasion for an expression of smugness, stand up, Perkins . . .No? Nothing? Perkins can find no reason for his expression of smugness. Rightly so, sit down, now, where were we? . . .Thank you, Hazel. The question was somewhat rhetorical, but I appreciate your intention In the beginning . . . was . . .

[*Pause. He makes idle noises with his mouth.*]

Before we continue I have an announcement to make; pay attention, please ... There is, as you may have heard, a vacant triangle in the percussion section of the school orchestra; anyone wishing to take advantage of—Nothing is gained, Beryl, by that kind of behaviour ... I *know* you have a penchant for the triangle, that goes without saying; you have a penchant for everything, Beryl—Green if you snigger again I may take strict measures. I think this is not an inopportune moment to explain to you, Beryl, that the reason you have such a penchant for so many things is that you *get* so *few* things, and the reason for that is that whenever you come across anything that interests you you frighten it away, Beryl, you scare it off by waving your arms above your head and screaming. I do have a certain amount of experience, and I tell you this: be it a butterfly, a fish, a triangle, or anything else, nothing was ever won by waving your arms about like a dervish and screaming 'Me, me, me.' As it is, I feel more inclined, if it comes to the choice, to give the triangle to Hazel here than to you, not because Hazel is keen, she isn't, she never is, Hazel is self-sufficient; but because she's *quiet*, Beryl. Now I don't say this with malice but—yes, I know it's unfair, but it's a fact of life. Be patient and it shall be given unto you ... If you wait long enough, Perkins, that goes without saying ... Whether you want to wait, Beryl is neither here nor there, and I'm not talking about triangles now, I'm talking generally ... So, those who wish to apply for the position of triangulist, hands up please. .. Higher, so I can see you ... Don't sulk, Beryl ... Beryl, I order you to put your hand up.

[*Pause.*]

One. We have one music-lover. Very well, Beryl, the position is yours ... The point of what, Brown? ... Brown, no one is forcing *you* to play the triangle, this is a free country—Green, you will go to the back of the class; you'll do shelter exercise for the rest of the period. Face the wall, hands on head. Now giggle at that . . . The fact is, Brown, your complete lack of interest in any of the school activities has not been lost on me. The school orchestra, the first-aid squad, the debating society— I am aware of that, Perkins, thank you; the point is that Brown showed not a spark of interest in the Debating Society even *before* it was disbanded . . . Disbanded, suppressed, let's not split hairs, Brown . . . Nonsense. How could you know beforehand it was going to be dis—. How *could* you know, *I* didn't know . . . Pessimism, Brown, is nothing to be proud of . . . Whether you were right or wrong is not the point . . . Brown, I'm not going to spend the period arguing the toss with you! . . . The fact remains, you show no interest in any of the extra-curricular activities, or the curricular ones for that matter, and I think this is deplorable. Because you're not unintelligent, Brown; you're not even self-contained by nature like Hazel here; this apathy of yours is an intellectual pose which you've picked up from certain adults who should know better. You try to excuse your behaviour by this hackneyed phrase about there being 'no future in it', but there *is* no excuse for apathy, and for two reasons: first, the future always has been uncertain and always will be; you think we're unique? . . . Total obliteration! Brown, you know nothing about it, leave it to those who do. Second, the value of an action has nothing to do with whether it has a future or not. The value of an action is in the doing of it, and if you ever *did* anything but sit with a cynical smile on your face you'd realise that. Ask the others, ask, ask . . . The value of playing the triangle is in the enjoyment of playing it, whether you or the triangle or the school orchestra or the school or anything else still exists to-morrow or not . . . Smith, please come out from under that desk!

[*Pause.*]

Was that you, Perkins? . . . Perkins, nobody would *want* to catch you playing the triangle; you have no sense of rhythm . . . You meant what? . . . You meant look what happened to Simpson? . . . Perkins, I may be losing my grasp of logic in my declining years, but the causative link between your musical disinclination and Simpson's unfortunate end escapes me. Eludicate for us, Perkins—Green, do go back to your place, I'm tired of looking at your back . . . Now, Perkins . . .

[*Pause.*]

Four, he was *four* months with the orchestra . . . And then his hair dropped out, yes . . . And then he died, yes . . .

[*Pause.*]

Are you suggesting it was *because* of his playing the triangle? . . . Everyone says so, and who's everyone? . . . This is quite incredible. Do you know, I had an idea you people were being *educated*; I had an idea you were learning science, technology; but when you come out with superstitious nonsense like— The fact *is*, Perkins, Simpson played the triangle; and Simpson unfortunately died; and that's all. I just say—Bassett, who's Bassett? . . . I don't recall any Bassett . . . Very well, if you say so, he played the triangle before Simpson . . . Then his hair dropped out? I'll take your word for it . . . Then he died, naturally . . .

[*Pause.*]

No, Perkins, I don't . . . How many deaths do I want, Brown? Brown, I can't stop you being cynical in a cynical world, but I *can* stop you being insolent.

[*On the last word he raps the desk with his cane. Slight pause.*]

Were there a dozen boys before Simpson or a hundred boys before Simpson or a *thousand* boys before Simpson it would mean nothing to me. I may be an old fogey on the verge of superannuation and the Old Teachers' Home, I may be kept here on sufferance to bore you with archaic and unscientific subjects like scripture and ancient history, but believe it or not I did learn a *little* science when I was a boy, because when I was a boy we learned a little of everything; I also dabbled in a subject called logic; and I know that magical powers are outside the scope of an orchestrial triangle . . . Neither could it attract radiation, Perkins, any more than could a—a—a *trombone*. Has the trombonist's hair dropped out, tell me? . . . Perkins? What? . . .

[*Pause.*]

This is all irrelevant. We are not unique . . . If you bothered to study history at all you'd see that. There was always something. There always has been something, there always will be something, floods, fires, plagues, road accidents, do you want to live for ever? The history of Man is the history of his escape— from disaster. He always survives; this is the interesting thing, this is the—ennobling fact. Always . . . The natural nobility in Man, and his inherent—ability to come . . . to come to his senses have always prevailed . . . in the end . . .

[*Pause.*]

People are dying all the time; one way or another. Whether they play the triangle or not. Sometimes they lose their hair first and sometimes they don't. The result is the same. It always has been. It's a fact of life. It's inevitable. There's nothing anyone can do about it.

[*Slight pause.*]

We must trust the authorities!

[*Slight pause.*]

Otherwise we have anarchy.

[*Slight pause.*]

And defeat.

[*Slight pause.*]

Democracy was built on the twin foundations of freedom of
the individual spirit and liberty to criticise. But it endures by
virtue of the willingness of its members to abrogate their rights
in time of stress. Temporarily. Till better times. Freedom
returns. Eventually. Intact . . . Almost . . .

[*Pause.*]

Wake that boy up . . . The boy at the end of the back row,
wake him up . . .

[*Pause.*]

Smith, I shall tell you for the last time. Come out from under
your desk . . . I can't hear what you're mumbling under
there . . . Flash? Nonsense, there was no flash. Learn to control
your imagination, Smith, use it for worthwhile purposes, use
it creatively—There is *no* sound. You imagined a sound; no
one ever hears it but you . . . If you must know, there would
be no sound. You'd not hear a sound, there would be no *time*
for a sound. Now sit at your desk. Ahead, Smith, not up, not
down. This is an order.

[*Slight pause.*]

There—is—no . . .

[*Pause. He picks up the exercise book.*]

H. Phipps, English Composition. 'My favourite sport . . . In
the beginning was hockey . . . ' Green, we may have the
opportunity of laughing at your attempt later . . . 'There was

also cricket, football and other sports there was also blocks of flats—' *Were*, Phipps, *were* 'blocks of flats large and small there was also dust boulders or rocks and small and large cliffs and precipices there was also the Atlantic Pacific and other oceans complete with fish and other denizens there was also land creatures with land to match there was also—' Punctuation, Phipps—'colours sounds and other senses thoughts and nameless horrors of all kinds.' Full stop, good. 'In the beginning there was everything that was going to happen be etc. and also there was everything that was not going to happen be etc. because if something is not going to happen or be that also is something only in a different way sometimes called the nether regions Hades etc. In the beginning it was all there and it was what you call a concept or Word and this concept or Word was like a ball surrounded by nothing only this nothing was also part of the Word and was in the ball and this ball stretched as far as you like to think only there was no such thing as stretched it was all in the ball which was full all the time until it opened like a bud only it was open all the time and time started only it was going all the time and it was all still in the ball . . . '

[*He throws down the book, sighs.*]

Out of a void grew a cloud, shading the bare parched places of the void from the glare of the void. From nothing comes nothing to shield nothing from nothing. Simpkins, have you an itch? . . . Stand up, Simpkins. Simpkins, I seem to remember asking you a question. I seem to remember asking you whether you had an itch, perhaps you would care to answer the question, Simpkins, have you an itch, Simpkins? . . . Simpkins has no itch, he assures us, he scratches but he has no itch. What do you seek to gain by it, Simpkins? . . . Simpkins doesn't know. He scratches without cause or purpose. Sit down Simpkins . . . I shall render a joke. In the beginning was the Word. The

parched lands nestled in the shade of existence, snigger later,
Green, the joke comes later. Immensity murmured, time
rippled, system crawled from nothing and staggered to its
knees; suns split, worlds cooled, lands rose, forest ground
forests underfoot. Sea bred slime bred cell bred creature,
horned, scaled, tailed, hoisting itself enormously ashore
millennium by millenium, for its tiny reason. Creature bred
creature. Life teemed. Horn split scale, feet split horn, club
split tooth. Till, kill, breath, breed, millenium by millenium.
Enter Man! Descends from the leafy refuge of the trees,
balances incredibly on two back feet, crushes all the
primitive forms who weighed themselves down with scales
and tails and horns and sabre-teeth, stands, alone, incredibly,
naked, defenceless, stretches himself erect and begins to claw
at the heavens!! . . . Simpkins, itchless, scratches. You may
laugh. You may all laugh, take advantage of the opportunity,
occasions are rare, seize it in both hands, you may laugh, you
may all laugh!!

[*His voice echoes. A pause.*]

Phipps. Stand up, Phipps. You were not laughing, Phipps.
Look at me, Phipps. Why were you not laughing, Phipps . . .
Phipps doesn't answer. What were you doing, Phipps? . . .
Phipps doesn't answer. I'll tell you what you were doing,
Phipps, you were crying, Phipps, you were not laughing but
crying, you are still crying, water is coming out of your eyes.
Time is short, Phipps, life is short, ours too, we are not unique,
there's no time for it, not now, do you hear me, do you
understand, there's *no time* for it!

[*Slight pause.*]

And no reason.

[*Slight pause.*]

All's for the best.

[*Slight pause.*]

As usual.

[*Slight pause.*]

We are taken care of.

[*Slight pause.*]

On the whole.

[*Slight pause.*]

Can one assume that having come so far along the road to our ultimate fulfilment, whatever that may be, we are to be abandoned by the authority we have selected for ourselves?

[*Slight pause.*]

Whichever happens, whatever come to pass, let us bear this in mind: there is that which has our best interests at heart; which takes care of us ... On the whole ...

[*Slight pause.*]

Did you hear something then, Smith ... ?

[*Slight pause.*]

We must have faith.

[*Slight pause.*]

Otherwise life becomes intolerable.

[*Slight pause.*]

Faith, courage—not the bluster of Hector but that quiet courage, that stillness of heart of which our race is not unjustly proud. Let us remember in the midst of our tribulations

—Smith, you have not been given permission to leave your—
Smith, I'm speaking to you, I'm informing you that—Come
back ,Smith!

[*Slight pause.*]

Yes, of course, close the door, Brown . . . And the rest of you
stop twittering. You are not birds. Birds twitter; you are not
birds . . . Phipps, for the last time, stop snivelling!

[*Slight pause.*]

In the beginning . . .

[*Slight pause.*]

What are you then? Simpkins, what are you? Green, Phipps,
Perkins, what are you, if you are not birds what are you . . . ?
You don't know? Then I'll tell you. You are not birds, not
ant-eaters, you'd better know while there's still time, not
hippopotami, not buffalo, you are members of the genus *homo
sapiens*, thinking man, reasoning man, logical man, you can
remember, you can anticipate, you can judge, you can condemn, you can oppose your thumb and your little finger; you
have ravaged the forests, irrigated the deserts, enslaved all
creatures, you are two million years old and you have
survived! . . . You have . . .

[*A Slight noise. Pause.*]

What about the dinosaurs, Brown? . . . I have no idea how
long the dinosaurs lasted, is it relevant how long the dinosaurs
lasted? The dinosaurs are dead . . .

[*Slight pause.*]

Where are you going? I said Brown, where are you—?
Perkins, Simpkins, where are you all going? Will you all go
back to your places, there is no cause for alarm, come back all

of you, kindly remember that you are—! One must have—!..

[*Long pause.*]

Well, Hazel?... Aren't you going with the rest?

[*Pause.*]

Close the door after you.

[*Pause.*]

Is it possible . . . is it just . . . is it barely possible that one's faith may have been . . . misplaced, that the authorities may be... may not be...

[*Pause. There is a sound, which increases.*]

That one is alone?... Dear children . . . In the beginning—was the... Word. And the Word... was—

[*There is a sudden silence.*]